TWENTY YEARS ON

Cricket's Years of Change
1963–1983

TWENTY YEARS ON

Cricket's Years of Change
1963 to 1983

Christopher Martin-Jenkins

WILLOW BOOKS
Collins
8 Grafton Street, London W1
1984

Willow Books
William Collins Sons & Co Ltd
London · Glasgow · Sydney · Auckland
Toronto · Johannesburg

First published 1984
© Christopher Martin-Jenkins 1984

BRITISH LIBRARY CATALOGUING IN PUBLICATION DATA

Martin-Jenkins, Christopher
Twenty years on.
1. Cricket—History—20th century
I. Title
796.35'86   GV913

ISBN 0-00-218087-1

Photoset in Linotron Sabon by
Rowland Phototypesetting Ltd
Bury St Edmunds, Suffolk
Made and printed in Great Britain by
Robert Hartnoll Ltd. Bodmin, Cornwall

CONTENTS

INTRODUCTION

'Limited-overs cricket has been the ruination of the great game.' Thus pontificated, in a voice loud enough to make Wilfred Rhodes stir in his grave, a former Yorkshire and England all-rounder in a bar one evening in 1983 – and there is nothing so pontifical, not even in Rome, as a Yorkshire cricketer in a bar. This one was speaking twenty years on from the introduction of limited-overs cricket into English county cricket and a few months before the dawning of 1984, George Orwell's year of doom.

Is cricket ruined, either as a game or a business? Or has it merely changed, as it has throughout its history, in tune with the times? What is certain is that the game has changed much more quickly in the last two decades, and more fundamentally at first-class level, than at any period since its popularity spread so fast through England and parts of the Empire in the second half of the nineteenth century.

It happens that the second volume of Altham and Swanton's classic *A History of Cricket* (Allen & Unwin) was published in 1962, a year before the introduction of the Gillette Cup. E. W. Swanton concluded at the end of the second volume that:

> 'The world of cricket makes an instinctive assessment of its heroes that is not wholly derived from the television cameras and the sporting pages. The future lies far less with the law-makers than with the men in the middle. The key to the health and prosperity of the game is embedded not in rules and regulations but in the hearts and minds of the cricketers of today.'

An essential question, therefore, in any assessment of the last two decades, is whether or not the players have been true to the spirit and tradition of their game. For it is the oldest

7

sporting cliché of all that the game is bigger than the players. Those players (at first-class level) certainly have a larger say in their own destinies in 1984 than they did in 1963. The Cricketers' Association, founded in 1968, soon established itself as a responsible union with a clear right to have a say in any proposed changes to the professional game in England. In Australia, however, with no tradition of cricket as a professional activity, change came violently with the Packer revolution of 1977. Essentially a battle over who should have the rights to televise Test cricket in Australia, Kerry Packer's crusade against the Australian cricket establishment (in which contemporary players had only recently and reluctantly been allowed a junior role) became also a 'just war' to win for the players a large share of the proceeds gained from their endeavours. Since his revolution involved radical changes to the whole mien of Australian cricket it led to clashes not just with the Australian establishment but with the English game as well. Imperceptibly, leadership in the game as a worldwide activity began to shift away from England to Australia. The hitherto ultra-conservative Australian Board changed rapidly into a body apparently prepared to try almost any gimmick if their commercial advisers told them there was money in it. Cricket's identification with dignity and tranquillity was replaced by seemingly endless controversy; moreover, the controversies have been gleefully fanned by the media at every opportunity.

After 1970 a cloud which until then had been 'no bigger than a man's hand' grew rapidly. Ever since it has hung over the world of cricket with a remorseless menace, occasionally dropping its contents and seldom allowing the sky to turn blue for long. That cloud, of course, is South Africa.

Patterns changed on the field as well during the years under review in these pages. England forsook the variety inherent in its cricket because of its climate and changed to covered wickets for county cricket, just as they had done for Test matches. Spin bowlers became less important throughout the world; in most countries the wrist spinner more or less dis-

appeared altogether. Test cricket became increasingly dominated by fast bowlers. Moreover, they were allowed to bowl
more bouncers more systematically, especially in the years
following Mr Packer's World Series Cricket promotions. Paradoxically, pitches tended to become slower in many countries
during the period. To counter the bouncers, batsmen took to
wearing helmets instead of caps; to counter the slower wickets,
they started using much heavier bats.

Captaincy became more 'scientific'. Field placings were
planned more carefully and adhered to more ruthlessly. Over-
rates became dramatically slower. Limited-overs cricket led to
new, less 'pure' batting techniques, more defensive bowling,
much improved outfielding. Limited-overs cricket itself became more common, and popular, in both amateur and
professional cricket in several countries. In England it helped
to keep county cricket vibrant and viable. Meanwhile international one-day cricket became a part of every tour: in Australia
the one-day internationals threatened the prestige of the Test
matches. Test cricket, however, proliferated to the extent that
the Tests were in danger of losing their sense of occasion, for
players and for spectators. At the heart of most of these
developments was the need to earn enough money to make a
successful business out of a sport. In an age of television and
many other counter-attractions, cricket no longer sold itself. It
had to be 'marketed'. But the marketing was not always done
by men and women who understood the game – either its
history or its longer-term interests.

These are some of the changes this book sets out to evaluate.
Some things still need to be changed, some changes need to be
reversed. In the short span of twenty years, certain events have
disrupted the game and its traditional virtues. For example:
tactics which may at best be called gamesmanship, at worst
cheating – including appealing when fielders know a batsman
is not out, bowling underarm sneaks, and slowing the over-
rate to deny batsmen runs and spectators entertainment;
swearing and public dissent towards umpires, including on
one occasion the physical abuse of a Test umpire; equally

boorish, indeed even more boorish behaviour by spectators, not just on the Sydney Hill but even in the Lord's pavilion; weak umpires who fail to appreciate the need to play cricket whenever it is possible to do so, or who fail to apply those laws which would check excesses by players; slow pitches, which help neither batsmen, nor fast bowlers, nor spinners; and gimmicks introduced by 'marketing men' and sponsors in the false belief that the game played properly is not an attraction in itself. Crowded international programmes have tired players and robbed important matches of their sense of occasion, both for players and spectators. Cricket has been used, too, as a means to achieve political ends which have very little to do with the game itself, thereby creating just the kind of bitterness between different races and countries that the same politicians seek in theory to eliminate.

Many of these developments have simply been reflections of wider trends in society, or the drift of world events, but others have been peculiar to cricket and, as we shall see, not all the undesirable changes are necessarily irreversible.

ONE

The Catalysts
Cricket in England in 1963

In 1963, the year of John F. Kennedy's assassination and the Great Train Robbery, there was a new Prime Minister in Britain following the Profumo scandal and a new Pope in Rome; it was also the year in which first-class cricket in Britain experienced two fundamental changes. The first, the abolition of amateur status, was significant, but more a reflection of changing attitudes in society than a radical shift in the character of cricket. The second may also be seen as a response to changing social habits: the introduction of the first limited-overs knockout competition. At the time it was a daring experiment, and one which, eventually, was to lead the rest of the cricket world by the ears – or by the pockets – into a new era of commercial cricket.

The Gillette company's patronage of the 'Knockout Trophy' was the first direct commercial sponsorship of county cricket as a whole. Their block grant to the counties that year amounted to a mere £6500, which was divided equally amongst the counties: today, that sum would only just cover the salary of one capped player in one county. (Whereas today's sponsorships are negotiated with a view to the under-writing of county cricket generally, this limited patronage from Gillette was considered only to be a guarantee against rain and subsequent loss of profits.)

Other issues debated at meetings before the start of the 1963 season indicated the strong mood for change that was in the air. They included the special registration of the future England batsman, Roger Prideaux, by Northamptonshire. Prideaux, formerly of Kent, later made a further move to

Sussex and there was to be a gradual, though carefully controlled, increase in the number of players moving counties in later years. The registration of overseas players was also discussed and their qualification period cut from three years to two. It would not be long before it became possible to register an overseas player without any residence in England at all, again with far-reaching consequences.

The Imperial Cricket Conference had decided in 1961 not to allow South Africa back into a membership they had lost because of their government's decision in May of that year to leave the Commonwealth. But at this stage South Africa (a founder member of the ICC along with England and Australia) remained a country whose international matches (against white countries only) were recognised as official Test matches. The Conference also agreed an experimental wording to the old Law 26, stating that a ball should not be 'jerked or thrown', and further decided that a front-foot no-ball law was the way to root out the fast bowler who 'dragged' his back foot well over the bowling crease. The issue of throwing and dragging was still very much a live one, especially in English minds, after the controversies of the 1958–59 series in Australia. But whilst cricket officials meeting as an international body were merely reacting to past events in their decisions, those in England were actually innovating. They had been forced, largely through financial hardship, to adapt or die.

The virtue of the Gillette Cup, indeed, was born of two necessities: the first was the financial crisis itself, common to most of the first-class counties in the early 1960s; the second was the need to inject some urgency into a county game which had become, if not moribund, at least stagnant.

It is often said that county cricket at this time was also uniformly dull, restricted by too much negative cricket, too many lifeless wickets, too many medium-paced seam bowlers prospering because conditions suited their type of delivery rather than that of real fast bowlers or genuine spinners. Batsmen concentrated on safety first, and did not play a ball unless they had to. But a glance at the first-class averages in

1962 rather tends to disprove the widely-held belief that county cricket had lost its character and its quality. The top seven in the batting averages were all players of undisputed Test class – including six of the finest players England has produced since the second world war. The top seven were Reg Simpson, Tom Graveney, Ted Dexter, Colin Cowdrey, Peter May, John Edrich and Ken Barrington. In 1983 only three batsmen qualified to play for England finished in the top ten. One was Cowdrey's uncapped son, Christopher. Another was Geoff Boycott, at the age of forty-two.

The bowling averages also suggest that quality was rising to the top, as it surely always will in any form of the game. Only two of the top fifteen were not Test cricketers, or not to become so. These two, David Sydenham of Surrey and Ossie Wheatley of Glamorgan (originally Warwickshire) were both genuine swingers of the ball. Five of the top fifteen were capable of truly fast bowling – Trueman, Larter, Rhodes, Loader and Flavell (perhaps also Les Jackson on some wickets) – but it is perhaps indicative of the type of cricket played that Tom Cartwright and Derek Shackleton both had good seasons as usual. Both were immensely accurate medium-fast seam and swing bowlers who became less effective against top-class players on good wickets. The most significant facts about the bowling averages of 1962, however, are that there was only one spinner – Sam Cook of Gloucestershire – in the top ten, and that only one overseas player achieved any prominence – the Australian Bill Alley. The nearest thing to the big, black fast bowlers who now abound in county cricket was Carlton Forbes of Notts, who took thirty-five wickets and frightened nobody.

Twenty years on another Cook, also a left-arm spinner, Nick Cook of Leicestershire, was the leading English wicket-taker. But he came only twenty-fifth in the national averages. Eight of the top ten bowlers of 1982 were qualified to play for countries other than England. In 1962 no fewer than twenty bowlers bowled more than a thousand overs in the season; in 1982 not one came near to doing so. The busiest bowler,

Cook, delivered 847.1 overs compared with the 1421.1 delivered by Don Shepherd of Glamorgan in the season two decades before. As it happened Cook was not a regular member of Leicestershire's one-day team, but even the busiest bowlers in all competitions in the 1980s are bowling less. The modern player would counter this suggestion that his predecessor was more active by pointing to the extra demands made on him by the constant shifting from one form of cricket to another. Most would also claim that the frequent journeys up and down motorways to fulfil county fixtures make the modern lifestyle much more wearing. But this particular argument was firmly despatched to the boundary in an article in *The Cricketer* by Trevor Bailey. (Some might say a finer attacking player with the pen than he was with the bat!)

> 'Before the motorways the travelling took much longer, over six hours from Essex for matches in the north and west. Every regular member in a county team next season (1983) can expect to play in 24 first-class cricket matches, 16 Sunday 'frolics' and say, on average, eight other limited-overs matches: approximately 96 days' cricket. I would normally play 34 first-class matches (102 days), send down over 1000 overs and have around 45 innings . . .'

Bailey also pointed out that the amount of overs bowled in each day's play in first-class cricket was substantially more – perhaps on average twenty more a day. But neither he nor his contemporaries would deny that first-class cricket in England in 1963 was becoming somewhat boring. This was certainly the view of the 'floating voters', who were staying away in their thousands. Increased television-watching and an increasing variety of counter-attractions, sporting and otherwise, for a more mobile and prosperous society to choose from resulted in steadily lower attendances at county games and, in most cases, declining figures for membership of county clubs. Most were making serious annual losses: necessity was pinching sharply.

There was no immediate agreement on adopting the Sunday

one-day matches which Rothmans began staging successfully after the formation of the Cavaliers in 1962. Instead county cricket's second knockout competition was started. The first, in 1873, had been abandoned after one match between Kent and Sussex. Ninety years later the first year of Gillette Cup cricket was a complete success: the sixty-five-over final at Lord's was the first all-ticket cricket match with every paid seat bought before the first ball was bowled. Thus 1963, the year that the amateur perished, was also the year in which commercial cricket was born.

TWO

One-Day Cricket
Whys, Wherefores, Pros and Cons

Even Messrs Sellar and Yeatman, the celebrated authors of
1066 And All That, would have been hard-pressed, after two
decades of limited-overs cricket played at professional level, to
decide whether or not this form of the game had been a 'good'
or a 'bad' thing. If one had to generalise in a sentence, one
might say that it has been good for the finances of the game but
bad for the standards of first-class cricket.

The success of the Gillette Cup quickly led to a proliferation
of one-day county cricket. Again the reasons were financial.
Crowds for the County Championship had been steadily
declining since the early years after the second world war
when, with people joyous at the freedom of being able to
watch cricket again, gates for county games alone approached
two million a year. By 1962 the overall attendance had
dropped to 933,000, with nine counties playing twenty-eight
matches and eight playing thirty-two.

The finances of county cricket will be looked at more closely
in the following chapter but it is necessary to qualify here the
often made statement that first-class cricket in England would
not have survived without one-day cricket. In the first place the
very rivalry of limited-overs cricket with three-day cricket has
accelerated the decline in attendances for the latter – down as
low as an average daily gate of 299 paying spectators in 1982
when a total of 156,181 people attended 522 days of Championship cricket. Secondly, one-day competitions, although
better attended, have not halted the overall decline in spectators at cricket matches in England. In 1975 the total paid
attendance at all Test and county cricket matches in England

16

was 1,235,000; by 1980 it had dropped to 974,000 and in 1982, following the Australian tour of 1981 which had pushed the overall figure back over the million mark again, the number had further plummeted to 782,909. In 1983, four Tests were watched by 175,684; a further 232,081 people watched the World Cup games; and the total attendance at county matches in four competitions was 444,141, excluding Middlesex, who did not return figures to Lord's. Essex, the champions, had 17,960 paying spectators at thirty-one Championship home days, compared with 13,300 for eight days of home play in the Sunday League.

It is a similar story in Australia where, to a much greater extent, crowds have been wooed to watch limited-overs cricket. To some extent this has been at the expense of Test cricket, but even more of Sheffield Shield matches. I well remember the start of play in a match between the England touring team and Australia's Combined Universities at the Adelaide Oval in 1979–80, the first year during which official Australian cricket was being professionally 'promoted'. When the first ball was bowled there were, excluding journalists, more players than spectators in that vast and beautiful ground. One thought of the old joke about the names of the spectators being announced to the players.

So long as it is kept apart from two-innings cricket, the limited-overs game, if it is played by top-class players, is unlikely to receive the same sort of slap in the face from an apathetic public. Though purists may disapprove of instant cricket and fear for the quality and standards of the game if it is played too often, there can be no denying its attractions.

Professional cricket in England, and to an increasing extent in Australia and other countries too, has become reliant on its income from television and sponsorship: the two go hand in hand. Both are attracted by the advantages of one-day cricket. The most important of these is that a result is guaranteed in a single day's play, weather permitting. A dull draw is impossible, although a dull match certainly is not. Some of the worst games are those when a team collapses early in a one-day

17

match or, alternatively, when the side batting second loses early wickets in pursuit of a large total. In these cases the possibility of a side holding on bravely for a draw does not exist and the matches lose their point. Some of the greatest and most exciting cricket matches ever have been draws – for example the Test matches at Brisbane and Adelaide in the famous Australian versus West Indies series of 1960–61.

Generally speaking, however, one-day cricket played by good players makes for an exciting spectacle. The more overs available to each side, the better the game, because the restrictions are fewer and the departures from the orthodox consequently less frequent. Whilst the result of these games is in doubt there is an essential urgency about them which is good for both participants and watchers: batsmen cannot afford to miss scoring opportunities, nor can captains, bowlers and fielders allow the batsmen liberties. Herein, also, of course, lies a weakness of the limited-overs game, because it thus encourages the defensive strategy in the field and outrageous departures from the principles of batting technique, which are usually fatal in the 'proper' game, certainly so in Test cricket. It is undoubtedly true that for a team to win a match, yet fail to bowl the opposition out, is a negation of the whole point of cricket as it was originally conceived and evolved.

Yet one-day cricket is often somewhat irrationally and dishonestly attacked. Whilst at first-class level it has changed and depurified many techniques, to the detriment of sound batsmanship; and the need to contain rather than to take wickets has encouraged the accurate, flat-flighted, slow bowler and the steady medium-pacer at the expense of the flighty spin bowler and the genuine fast bowler, nevertheless much of the cricket played has had a vital quality often missing before. Fielding standards have improved to heights of athletic brilliance once extremely rare – now every other professional cricketer is a Jessop, a Hobbs or a Constantine – and batsmen have in many cases discovered a freedom and power of stroke they would not otherwise have been forced to use. Glenn Turner is the classic exception to the rule that limited-overs cricket tends to lead batsmen into bad habits. He was a cramped and limited batsman when first he came to Worcestershire from New Zealand. But in one-day games he became a virtuoso player of great versatility, who dictated to the bowlers rather as Bradman used to do in Test matches – though with some strokes, like the 'chip' over the inner ring of defensive fielders, that even Bradman did not employ. Such was the beneficial effect of the freedom of one-day cricket that Turner was then able to dominate rather than just to survive in first-class cricket as well, becoming only the second non-Englishman to score a hundred hundreds.

At amateur level, where one-day as opposed to limited-overs cricket has always been the staple fare, the arrival of restricted-overs cricket has tended to have similar effects: more batting enterprise confronted by less variety in the field. To play it is often enjoyable and exciting. To say it is not real cricket is rubbish: it is simply a different form of cricket from that played over a longer time-scale. Good cricketers will thrive in both. But my experience of club cricket is that it has become more defensive, tactically speaking, because of the limited-overs mentality. Too many captains instruct their bowlers to contain first, take wickets second. Too many batsmen try to survive rather than look for runs.

Most of the major cricketing countries now have one-day knockout competitions. In Australia, for instance, it is the Macdonalds Cup, in New Zealand the Shell Cup, in South Africa the Datsun Shield, in West Indies the Geddes Grant/ Harrison Line Trophy, formerly the Gillette Cup. India and Pakistan have so far resisted the temptations, partly because of the vast distances between the main clubs and zones, but both now build at least three one-day internationals into their domestic programmes. No country has nearly as much one-day cricket at the top level of domestic competition as we do in England. As already discussed, the Gillette Cup was introduced in 1963, starting as a sixty-five-over contest but quickly being reduced to one of sixty. Now the NatWest Bank Trophy, the competition has produced consistently good and exciting cricket, and from the outset has never attracted less than a full house to the final at Lord's in September. The most famous match in the Gillette was probably the 1971 semi-final at Old Trafford when, because of a shower at lunchtime, play continued until 8.55 pm and finished in a decidedly murky twilight with a dramatic onslaught by David Hughes, who took 24 off one over of off-spin from John Mortimore. Gloucestershire's main strike bowler was Mike Procter, who still had three overs of his quota of twelve left when the climax of the game was reached. Had the Gloucestershire captain, Tony Brown, called him back into the attack earlier instead of allowing Mortimore to continue his spell for one more fatal over, the umpires, 'Dicky' Bird and Arthur Jepson, would have had to make a delicate decision as to whether to bring the players off for bad light and take the game into the anti-climax of a second day. The story goes, in any case, that after a consultation with the Lancashire captain, Jack Bond, David Hughes quietly appealed against the light soon after his arrival at the crease. Arthur Jepson took Hughes to one side at the end of the over, told him to look up at the sky and report what he could see.

'I can see the moon', said Hughes.

'Well 'ow much further do you want to see?' inquired Arthur in his deep, north-country drawl.

Gillette withdrew from their sponsorship after 1980 because their market research revealed that more people were associating Gillette with cricket than with razor blades. Here was proof both of the power of cricket and of the effectiveness of sports sponsorship.

The advent of the National Westminster Bank (who paid an index-linked £250,000 a year for the right to lend their name to the competition, as opposed to Gillette's original £6500) was rewarded with a sensational first final in 1981 in which Derbyshire scrambled a single off the last ball of their sixty overs to win by virtue of losing fewer wickets in a tie.

The success of the knockout cup soon led to more limited-overs cricket in England. In 1969 the tobacco company, John

Player, began their sponsorship of a new Sunday league of forty overs per side, starting after lunch on Sundays and providing an ideal form of instant cricketing entertainment for the undiscerning spectator. There was no time for anyone except the opening batsmen to 'build' an innings and restrictions abounded: only eight overs were allowed as the maximum for each bowler; the bowler's run-up was restricted to fifteen yards; and, later, restrictions were made in the field, too, when the idea of a thirty-yard circle inside which a certain number of fielders (in this case four) must always be when each ball is bowled, was imported and adapted from Australia. More of this anon.

The forty-over game became an art in itself, with inventive stroke-players and fleet-footed fielders at even more of a premium. Because it was easy for people to come to watch on Sunday afternoons, and because some big hitting and a result were guaranteed in the 'family package', the Sunday league quickly established its own enthusiastic public.

The BBC televised the competition from the start, which ensured that the sponsors got value for their money. John Player will have given three million pounds to cricket when their present contract expires in 1986. In 1969 the prize money they offered was £9550. By 1984 it had risen to £64,700. Crowds for the competition reached a peak of 374,000 in 1975. By 1982 the attendances had fallen to 189,900 for 133 days overall – an average Sunday crowd of 1428. In 1983 the total was 190,739. The competition had lost its novelty and counter-attractions of both a sporting and non-sporting kind were increasing. Crowds were often much bigger for a Lord's Taverners charity match, in which the cricket was almost incidental and the star names – former cricketers, actors, footballers, television personalities – were the draw. Thus there is some evidence that the 'new' spectators, attracted initially to one-day cricket because it was relatively brief, more instantly appealing and guaranteed to produce a result, were starting to fall away in the 1980s. Nevertheless the John Player League remains popular and if

Championship (three-day) cricket were to be substituted, Sunday crowds would, I fear, fall.

England's third major competition, the Benson and Hedges, started in 1972 and was something of a mixture of the earlier competitions. The overs-limit was fifty-five, with bowlers limited to eleven overs each. The knockout stage was not reached until eight survivors had been determined by round-robin leagues in four geographical zones. Although this was a more equitable system than the straight knockout formula of the Gillette, the five fewer overs in the Benson and Hedges matches made for that much less satisfactory cricket – and, for no better reason than mere chance, the matches at the knock-out stage of the competition, especially in the finals at Lord's, seldom reached the same dramatic heights. At last, in 1983, the sponsors were rewarded with a genuine nail-biter when Middlesex somehow beat Essex by four runs in a match finishing at 8.50 pm.

The Benson and Hedges competition, incidentally, was the first in England to adopt and adapt the excellent Australian idea of a circle of discs placed thirty yards from the wickets, inside which a certain number of fielders must remain throughout the match. There are variations on the regulations applying to these circles, but the best of them, now used for all limited-overs competitions in England, states that four fielders, plus the bowler and wicket-keeper, must be inside the circle when the ball is delivered. Until the introduction of circles, the standard practice was for several, and sometimes all, fielders to be placed on the boundary during the closing stages of an innings, thus limiting shots which would normally have brought four runs to only one or two.

Since there are so many limitations already in the one-day game, it would be no bad thing in my view to dictate not just how far from the wickets fielders should be but also on which side of the wickets. I would like to see a limit of six, or even of five, on one side. This would remove the dreadful sight of batsmen moving to the leg-side in order to counter a heavily biased leg-side field and endeavouring to drive, carve or slash the ball through the gaps on the off. A few players – Keith Fletcher and Viv Richards perhaps in particular – are capable of employing this particular unorthodoxy with a fair degree of success. But for the majority the result, sooner or later, is inevitable: a whirl of the bat followed a split-second later by falling timber. I have had the experience of taking my sons to watch limited-overs games and trying to explain why so many batsmen step away to leg when they, like all young players, have been told that to do this rather than to stay in line with the ball should be fatal.

The artificiality does not end with the batsman. The bowler operating to a leg-side field is naturally obliged to bowl a leg-stump line, and when batsmen try to counter this by moving to leg, the temptation for bowlers, especially in the later stages of an innings, is to follow the batsman and aim the ball at his legs. Richards countered this tactic memorably in the 1979 World Cup Final by twice moving to the off during the last over from Hendrick and lifting the ball over square-leg for six. But Richards is a law unto himself. Otherwise, every Sunday, and frequently in other one-day matches, first-class cricketers are reduced to village-green crudities. It is the fault not of the players (although very often more orthodox bowling and batting would be equally, or more, effective) but of the type of cricket they are obliged to play.

Some of the best limited-overs cricket at first-class level has been seen in internationals, notably in the three World Cups sponsored by Prudential Assurance in 1975, 1979 and 1983. The matches were played over sixty overs, starting at 11 am in the first year and at 10.45 am in the latter two – largely a reflection of the slower over-rates which had become habitual in big-match cricket throughout the 1970s, as captains agonised over their field-placings and bowlers took their time.

Many of these games were long drawn out: in 1983 games beginning at 10.45 frequently went beyond 8.00 in the evening. Often the result was predictable soon after lunch, either because one side had failed to get enough runs at a fast enough rate on a good wicket, or because they had scored so many at such a rapid rate that the fielding side were clearly in with little chance of overhauling them. But, generally speaking, all three competitions were outstanding for the standard of the cricket played, and of the entertainment provided. The West Indies were supreme in the first two World Cups, losing not a single game and looking seriously like doing so on only one occasion. This was in one of the first-round matches in the first year when Pakistan, then as now a powerful batting side, scored 266 for seven in their sixty overs, with fifties from Mushtaq Mohammad, Majid Khan and Wasim Raja. Twice West Indies appeared to be hopelessly placed, losing their eighth wicket at 166 and their ninth at 203. Then, however, two of their most phlegmatic cricketers, Deryck Murray and Andy Roberts, added 64 to win the match with only two balls to spare. In such games as these the one-day game is every bit as good as the two-innings variety and there have been many such frenzied and thrilling finishes over the years.

The famed unpredictability or, if you prefer, the 'glorious uncertainty', of the game was never better demonstrated than in the 1983 final between West Indies and India. India had earned their place at Lord's by virtue of wins against West Indies, Australia and, in the semi-final, England. But few expected them to extend West Indies on the great day and fewer still after India had managed to score only 183. West Indies, with Viv Richards at his superlative best, were 50 for one. But after hitting seven fours, Richards was caught by India's captain, Kapil Dev, a swirling catch held by the man of the hour. Thereafter, amidst palm-sweating tension, India's medium-paced bowlers wormed their way slowly through all the famous names in the West Indies team. They won in the end by 43 runs, but only when the number eleven, Holding, was out, did one believe their improbable victory would really happen. The following winter West Indies played five limited-overs internationals in India and won the lot!

In 1983, partly in order to try to make a larger profit from the World Cup than in the first two years when the proceeds, because of vast overhead expenses (not least the travel and hotel expenses of the competing teams) did not match the widespread appeal, each country played the other twice rather than once in the first round in order to determine the semi-finalists. Perhaps because there were eight teams involved, however, one did not get the same feeling of overkill that one has felt about the triangular tournaments which have been played in Australia since the 1979 agreement between the Australian Cricket Board and Kerry Packer's company, PBL, which included a clause catering for a large number of one-day internationals. No matter how good the players involved, or indeed how good some of the matches themselves, I personally found my appetite for cricket cloyed by the prospect of seeing the same teams play each other over and over again. In 1982–83, Australia, England and New Zealand each played ten games to decide who should go through to a best-of-three-matches final. It would have been best-of-five if the Australian authorities had had their way. Originally, all this was largely for the benefit of television. Yet – so far at least – the matches have not lost their appeal to the home spectators. A total of 551,465 people clicked through the turnstiles to watch seventeen internationals in 1982–83, compared with 538,601 who watched the twenty-five days cricket in the five Test matches between Australia and England. On the other side of the coin, however, a year later two of the country's most successful players, Greg Chappell and Rodney Marsh, both gave the plethora of internationals as one of their main reasons for retiring.

The fashion for one-day cricket in Australia (at first they had pooh-poohed the game as 'unreal cricket') has led the way in the general proliferation of international cricket. New Zealand, for example, found themselves involved in nineteen such internationals against Australia, England and Sri Lanka between January and April 1983. Crowds for these internationals everywhere are good and the profits they make are important to the well-being of the game. But the players and the spectators will grow tired of too much of the same. Far better to leave them wanting more rather than to drive them away eventually by failing to offer variety.

This was the verdict not just of Chappell and Marsh, but also of Bill O'Reilly, one of Australia's greatest spin bowlers. He has been a harsh critic of the one-day game in his country:

> 'This game is injecting a dementia into the souls of those who play it. People seem prepared to watch batsmen get out in strange ways. It was sad to see a player like Kim Hughes dance down the wicket in Brisbane (January, 1982) and get stumped having a wild swing. It was a sacrifice of all the natural talent he has in him. In years to come that can be played back and used as evidence: it's character assassination. The same has happened to Greg Chappell ... and even Dennis Lillee does not try to bowl fast. Jeff Thomson is the only bowler I have seen try to bowl fast in this ridiculous game that seems to be all about containment rather than taking wickets. It has driven tradition away from the game.' (*Sydney Morning Herald*)

Certainly the old traditions mean less, techniques have been changed, and elegance and variety lost. Great players have been made to look ordinary and ordinary players made to look better than they are. On the other hand a game once considered staid, slow and boring by those who did not understand it has been given a bright new 'pop' image and attracted a new audience, much of it young. At least some of them may be inspired to learn about the more subtle forms of the game by first being attracted to its limited-overs version, just as many are attracted eventually to classical music having first tasted the more basic attractions of rock or jazz. As for the players, improved fielding and a greater range of attacking shots have been some compensation for declining technical standards.

THREE

County Cricket
Since 1963

The administration of cricket in the United Kingdom has been considerably reformed in the last twenty years, during which MCC, the owners of Lord's, have lost both theoretical and practical power over the first-class game. Once the oracle of world cricket, MCC is now merely the game's most important club, though still it retains control over the most famous of all grounds and remains guardian of the Laws, as well as providing the chairman and secretary of the International Cricket Conference. Though diminished, their influence is still strong. Personal rivalries amongst the senior staff at Lord's have exacerbated the differences which resulted from the setting up in 1968 of a new supreme body in English cricket, the Cricket Council, the *sine qua non* for attracting some government money to cricket. The new Council was largely made up of representatives from three bodies: MCC; the newly-formed Test and County Cricket Board (responsible for first-class cricket and replacing the old Board of Control); and another new body, the National Cricket Association (which has responsibility for all non-first-class cricket in the United Kingdom). Initially, each body had five members on the Council. Gradually the power of the TCCB, which runs the cricket which brings in the money, has, according to the premise that he who pays the piper calls the tune, become pre-eminent. The Cricket Council does little more than rubber-stamp what the TCCB has decided and in 1982 the representation of the TCCB on the Council was in any case increased to eight members, compared with MCC's three and NCA's five.

G. O. Allen, formerly captain of England, Chairman of Selectors, and President as well as long-serving Treasurer of MCC, promptly resigned to protest at this 'takeover' of all English cricket, by a body originally intended to represent only the first-class game.

Apart from the new one-day competitions begun in 1963, 1969 and 1972, and the 1968 decision to allow the immediate registration of an overseas player every three years, the major changes in county cricket have been representative of attempts to make the Championship game more attractive to the public – a public which still follows it eagerly in newspapers and on the air, but which does not have the time and inclination to attend matches. In 1974, for example, an experiment began in which the first innings of any Championship game was limited to 100 overs, with an equal number of bonus points available to batsmen who scored at a reasonable rate and bowlers who took wickets. (Bowlers' points were gained for three, five, seven and nine wickets taken in the first 100 overs and batsmen's points for 150, 200, 250 and 300 runs in the first 100 overs.)

On the whole, these incentives worked. Teams were forced to attack in the field if they wanted bowling points and to bat with a proper sense of purpose. But there were snags too. It was still possible to bowl to contain the batsmen, as in limited-overs cricket, rather than to try to get them out, hoping instead that they would destroy themselves in the search for batting points. Moreover, those batsmen coming in in the middle order often had to have a quick bash in the hope of winning an extra point after the opening batsmen had taken their time to build the foundation of the innings. Often, too, the middle-order men were the promising young English players, following in the wake of the big star or stars from overseas who occupied the prime places in the batting order. For English Test cricket this was bad, and any extra spectators attracted to county cricket itself by the overseas experts were probably lost to Test cricket because England were not thought to be worth paying to watch unless they were winning matches impressively. On the other hand, however, some of England's opponents, notably the West Indies, but also New Zealand and Pakistan, became more formidable, and therefore more attractive, opponents because so many of their players became more mature as a result of experience gained in county cricket.

In 1983 the Cambridge, Sussex and England batsman, Paul Parker, put forward in *The Cricketer* magazine, and also in a talk to The Cricket Society, his theory that England's modest performances in international cricket in recent years have been partly attributable to the fact that county cricketers play an undesirable amount of cricket. His solution was a Championship between sixteen counties (wisely he did not specify which one would be eliminated) divided into two groups of eight, each of the teams playing the others in their zone once, with the winners of the groups playing each other in a 'grand final'. Matches would be played over four days, from Friday to Monday, involving only nine weekends of the summer. The John Player League would be scrapped and two one-day competitions (under the present sponsors, the Nat West and Benson and Hedges) would be played on the other weekends, with Test matches filling the remainder.

Amongst the advantages Parker mentioned for such a system were that groundsmen could prepare better wickets, county players would be drawn from club leagues which would thus improve the leagues' standard, players would be fresher, and, with fewer playing opportunities, better able to apply themselves on the big occasion. There would also be a wider pool for Test selectors to choose from, because under the present system some talented cricketers are not prepared to take the gamble of a career in the game. Above all, in Parker's view, players would be only part-time professionals, able to do another job almost full-time throughout the year. With so much Test cricket now being played, this would hardly be feasible for the leading players, but for the rest his hypothesis is worth considering.

Parker's thesis is based on what he believes to be the strong possibility of financial ruin for many counties and the idea that, for county cricketers themselves, his system would be more secure (assuming they have a year-round job to fall back on) and more enjoyable.

His proposed system is, of course, similar to the one used in most of the other Test-playing countries. The irony is that in Australia, by increasing the amount of international cricket played since 1979, the traditional system of part-time players emerging from grade cricket to State and Test level has been replaced recently by one which demands that the top players commit themselves to the game on a fully professional basis. Greg Chappell said, on his retirement in 1984, that the modern international cricketer could not be expected to play and at the same time hold onto an outside job and a marriage – 'perhaps one, but not both'. (*Melbourne Age*)

In England, there is no doubt that Parker's ideas would be an improvement in many ways. But cricket has been played professionally at county level for more than a century and since 1963 all county players have been professionals. Too many people have too many interests vested in the present structure for the clock to be put back to the days of the nineteenth century when the majority of players were amateur, able by either private means or because of generous employers to play cricket for their counties almost as often as they wished, and when international commitments for the leading players were far fewer. Even in those days county clubs had seasons when financial anxiety pressed hard on the administrators. Nowadays every decision taken by the officials and committees of county clubs has a financial aspect to take into account. In short, county cricket since 1963 has become obsessed by the need to keep itself solvent.

The introduction of talented overseas players and the increase in the number of trophies competed for has meant that no county match, under whatever rules it is being played, is ever a foregone conclusion these days – as, for example, Yorkshire versus Somerset in the 1930s or Surrey versus Sussex in the 1950s would have been. Domination by a few clubs is a thing of the past. Though limited-overs cricket, played as often as it is, has depurified batting techniques and discouraged genuine fast bowling or subtle, flighty spin, to the detriment of English Test cricket, it has undoubtedly enabled many more players to have their hour of glory for the county. Moreover, the policy in all the counties, except Yorkshire, of allowing an outstanding cricketer from overseas to fill a prime batting or fast bowling place has prevented any team from going into any match with an inferiority complex. Often these players – for example, Eddie Barlow at Derbyshire or Mike Procter at Gloucestershire or Richard Hadlee at Nottinghamshire – have had a beneficial effect on the young English players around them. More often, unfortunately, they have denied opportunities to promising home-bred cricketers who would have developed faster given those opportunities. To give but two recent examples, Kim Barnett of Derbyshire improved rapidly when the South African, Peter Kirsten, left Derbyshire in 1983, and Tony Pigott of Sussex proved himself something more than just another trundler when Imran Khan of Pakistan was unable to bowl for Sussex in the 1983 season because of a leg injury (and in the previous season, too, because of an overseas tour).

Techniques and tactics may have altered greatly in the last twenty years but the county game still provides cricket of high quality – though few who watched county cricket before the last war, or the lingering few who saw it before the first, will agree. The standard remains very high in batting, even if most of the best players come from outside England. There are now many more genuinely fast bowlers, making batting for a living a hazardous profession, though there are far fewer spinners of any real quality and batsmen therefore succumb to the best of them much more easily than once they did. With leg-spinners almost extinct, the Pakistani, Abdul Qadir, wrought havoc amongst the counties on the Pakistan tour of 1982. A year later, two 'ancient' left-arm spinners, Norman Gifford, aged forty-three, and Derek Underwood, aged thirty-eight, both exceeded 100 wickets.

Fielding, as all are agreed, is vastly more athletic than it was and, generally, fielders are more carefully and ruthlessly placed by captains. (It is, altogether, a more ruthless game. Captains do not last long any more if their team is not successful.) Much imagination and enterprise certainly went with the amateurs, but so, too, did some indifferent cricketers who might not have played county cricket on merit. To a certain extent the best overseas players have filled the void left by the best amateurs. The problem since the 1970s has been that too many of the chosen few stay on to become permanent fixtures in the county sides, eventually qualifying as technically 'English'. Thus the county is able to engage another ready-made potential match-winner from overseas rather than waiting more patiently for its own home players to develop.

Matchwinners many of the overseas stars certainly have been. But if success on the field has been common to all seventeen counties and has been chased with increasing fervour by most of them – sometimes, as in Yorkshire, almost to the point of desperation – financial worry has also been shared by them all. Towards the end of the period under review the losses incurred by some counties were reaching alarming proportions. In 1982 Lancashire lost £151,000, Glamorgan £84,000 and Gloucestershire £70,000. Careful husbandry improved the position of all three the following year, but none could afford complacency. No longer can wealthy local patrons dig into their pockets to bale the clubs out at times of crisis as once they did (for money worries are as old as county cricket itself). Now even wealthy local firms need to be convinced of the worthiness of the cause: and they are a good deal less altruistic than private patrons of old.

Seldom, if indeed ever, has county cricket paid for itself. Gate money now accounts for only about a tenth of the income of the average county in an average season. Membership subscriptions comfortably exceed gate money but still leave the counties far short of the income required to meet the cost of wages, administration and maintenance of club grounds. In 1982, for example, Lancashire made only £44,000 in gate money, yet they had to pay out £215,000 to players, £54,000 to ground and maintenance staff and £60,000 to secretarial staff. Moreover, their huge loss was made despite having a membership of 11,458, more than Yorkshire, and far more than any of the other fifteen counties.

The two major sources of income for any county club, apart from gate receipts and membership, are the annual handout from the TCCB (made up of sponsorship, broadcasting fees and receipts from Tests and one-day internationals) and locally engendered funds, such as advertising on the grounds owned or used by the clubs, local sponsorship and catering. By far the largest item in the annual budget is the income from the TCCB which, of course, varies considerably from year to year – according to the attractiveness of the country touring England, and the profits they create for the TCCB once the expenses and guaranteed profit, always agreed in advance, has been paid to the visitors.

In 1981, Botham's *annus mirabilis*, the TCCB income from gates, sponsorship and television was three million pounds. A year later this had dropped by half a million pounds, a decline entirely attributable to the lesser attraction, in the public's view, of the Indian and Pakistani teams by comparison with Australia. Crowds for the six Tests of 1981 totalled 380,546; for India and Pakistan three games against each country produced total crowds, respectively, of 93,878 and 144,354. Four Tests between England and New Zealand in 1983 produced 175,684 spectators, including members. Thus there was less to go round for the counties. On the other hand, the 1983 revenue was large, £823,590 from the Tests being augmented by a share of the £1,195,712 coming from the Prudential World Cup gate receipts.

About ninety per cent of the TCCB income, after expenses, goes to the first-class counties, with those clubs whose grounds are used for Tests receiving an extra share of the profits. But the counties have had to find increasingly diverse ways of reducing their own losses. Warwickshire's Supporters Association led the way with the famous Warwick (Football) Pool, an original idea, and lotteries, run by the county clubs with tickets sold through agents or volunteers, have also proved a valuable source of income. Sponsors are found for various functions, even such modest ones as paying for the teams' meals and providing the ball for the match.

Business entertaining at county grounds, most of which have now developed much-improved facilities for watching the game in comfort, with food and drink to hand, has become common. Essex, for example, whose secretary, Peter Edwards, was chosen for the job because he was an expert in business administration, have their facilities at Chelmsford – and special marquees at other grounds – used by some 300 local companies each season. Even if only a handful of spectators arrive to watch a midweek Championship match, therefore, the club is usually assured of at least a modest profit. Lancashire, Gloucestershire (in partnership with Phoenix Assurance, who bailed them out when bankruptcy was imminent), Somerset, Sussex (who have their own pub, though it has seldom made the profit it should) and Hampshire are all counties with good modern accommodation for functions such as dinners and wedding receptions. This enables these counties to make at least some winter use of grounds which were once white elephants when the season ended. Most counties now also have indoor nets at their main ground, catering for the many club cricketers who like to keep a bat in their hands in the winter – and also for the coaching of schoolboys.

Each county now has its supporters club and the sale of lottery tickets, books, journals, ties, badges and souvenir material all brings in useful income as well as encouraging participation by local communities in the activities of the club. Surrey's professionally-run marketing department now produces twice as much income for the club as gates and membership.

The best gate receipts returned by any county in 1983 were those of Kent, whose 36 home days of Championship cricket produced 18,997 paying spectators, an average of only 528 a day.

Despite all the enterprises, great and small, many of those involved fully in the administration of county cricket feel that it is still outdated. Instead of the cumbersome committees of old, with various sub-committees, the advocates of more modern management methods would prefer a Chief Executive in charge of a trim committee, answerable not to the membership of the club but to a board of directors. In other words the sport should be recognised for the business that it now is.

That is fine, so long as the cricketing interests of each club remain paramount. The most vital committee in any club is the cricket committee itself, dealing exclusively with playing matters. Some clubs have got it right: Middlesex, for example. Charles Robins, son of R.W.V., is in charge of the cricket committee, with Don Bennett as the county coach, and between them they make the most of the considerable young talent in the Middlesex area. Much of this originates from the West Indian immigrants to Britain in the 1950s and 1960s: Norman Cowans is a prime example. Chairman and coach also work closely with the county captain who, in the case of Mike Brearley and now of Mike Gatting, is largely in control of team selection and policy. Yet Middlesex also has its problems. Two secretaries left in the space of three years in the early 1980s, mainly because their hands were tied by too many committees.

The fortunes of Yorkshire in the last decade present an unfortunate and well-publicised picture of county cricket. A large, unwieldy, often divided general committee; a cricket committee with, apparently, too little weight; and several different captains, one of whom, Geoff Boycott, felt he had to write to *The Times* to reveal the intrigues and the efforts by committee members (let alone team members) to stab him in the back. I will return a little later to the painful subject of Yorkshire's civil war.

Generally, my own feeling is that those who advocate trimmer and more business-like management of county clubs are right, but only to a point. Once the goodwill and voluntary involvement of cricket followers willing to help is lost, there is a danger of dehumanising a sport which has always thrived on the tremendous affection, of all those involved, for the game of cricket itself.

All counties need to keep close links with those playing cricket in their area. The best way to do so would be for the county club itself, with voluntary help, to organise the club leagues – preferably linking the sponsors of these leagues to their own county sponsorship – and to encourage the natural progression of promising schoolboy players into a suitable club and, if good enough, on to the playing staff.

Christopher Bazalgette, a club cricketer in Hampshire with considerable expertise in the fields of advertising and marketing, recently produced a blueprint for the running of a modern county club, utilising both the skill of professionals and the goodwill of amateur cricket followers. 'It is very evident,' he says, 'that not enough respect has been paid to the customer. The attitude has been "we offer you cricket; please come and watch". Instead, the counties must ask what they have to do to persuade families to watch cricket in the face of increasing competition from other leisure activities. Any business has to be advertised, sold, researched, improved.'

Bazalgette took Hampshire CCC as an example, listing the club's assets and suggesting how it should be run.

GENERAL

If county cricket is to survive as its own master, the counties participating in the first-class game have to become self-financing – which, in most cases, means a complete reappraisal and changed approach. No longer can a county hope that cricket alone will attract enough supporters/members to finance the 1st and 2nd XIs and their administration.

Each county must run itself as a business – requiring departments such as:

1. Financial   2. Sales   3. Marketing
4. Administration   5. Personnel   6. Training

Plus specifically:

  a. Sponsorship b. Supporters   c. Advertising
  d. Fund raising   e. Commercial enterprises.

AN APPRAISAL OF HAMPSHIRE CCC

Facilities

1. Head Office: Southampton – own ground, comprising:
   a. A ground b. Indoor school   c. Parking area
   d. Excellent new catering centre/squash courts
   e. Pavilion plus bars f. Seating/stands – dilapidated   g. Matting nets   h. A small museum/library.
2. The use of Bournemouth and Portsmouth grounds.
3. Players: attractive team of good potential.

The County – Market/customers

1. This county has many leagues and hosts of clubs, schools and wandering sides playing cricket.
2. There is also excellent press, radio and TV support for the game.
3. Administratively there are a great many professional people with experience in marketing and sales promotion who would willingly give time and expertise to help the county club, if they were asked so to do and if their advice and efforts are used.

At present, there is little incentive for club cricketers either to watch or support their county. If they do attend, what is there for the wife or girlfriend, son, daughter or baby? What facilities to feed and change baby, or to keep all the family amused?

The Competition

1. The beaches – for *all* the family.
2. The countryside – New Forest.
3. Fetes/shows throughout the summer.
4. Other cricket/tennis/gymkhanas/sailing/walking.
5. Safari parks etc.

ONE ANSWER

with many suggestions – which could be taken as a whole or in part

Organisation

a. The Secretary – Chairman – President – Captain + two others (possibly one financial adviser, one marketing adviser)
   This to be the senior committee (holding company)
b. Selection committee
c. A financial committee (voluntary)
d. Marketing/sales team (voluntary)
e. Supporters team (voluntary)
f. Commercial enterprise team (voluntary)
g. Sponsorship/fund raising team (voluntary)

The Holding Company would run the club, with the aid of the other groups, with whom they would discuss regular reports on progress within the respective disciplines of each task force – they would co-opt representatives depending on the necessary requirements/ targets at hand – but it would be mandatory for the Holding Company to make decisions, based on the reports offered to them. There would be a quorum of three who could make urgent decisions, should urgency be the key to success. It is imperative that Hampshire recognise that, at the moment, they have a very small package to offer would-be supporters. Facilities, although much improved, with a new catering centre, are still lacking in other ways.

It is suggested that immediately one man is allocated the task of liaison with cricket leagues and clubs *throughout* the county, with an ultimate goal that the administration of leagues should be headed by the county administrator. Thus the *focal point* of cricket would be Southampton and cricketers would become used to visiting and contacting the county ground.

The county club should wish to become friends with all club players, at all levels, and to market its services to the clubs, gaining their support. It would need to be a two-way operation – support from the county for coaching, after-dinner speeches, presenting awards etc. The operation to be financed by a small levy paid by leagues and clubs.

The ground buildings need to be repaired, cleaned and painted. Schools to be contacted – teams of boys earning the privilege of meeting the players, watching nets, receiving autographs etc, for their help in keeping the facilities in good order. There must be many who would love such an opportunity, and it would also give the boys an incentive, to make them feel part of the 'team' i.e. their county club.

The supporters – to have a supremo who sets up groups throughout the county:
1. Bournemouth 2. Southampton 3. Portsmouth
4. Basingstoke 5. Stockbridge 6. Farnborough
with duties such as: fund raising, collecting parties to attend matches, a supporters club and prizes for sub-groups competing for inter-area recognition (including badges, involvement with the teams etc). A supporters' newsletter. Incentives for recruitment etc.

Marketing/sales
A selected team of professional marketeers/salesmen who would prepare methods to market the club and its facilities. To promote ways of fund raising, sponsorship, special events from a corporate and regional point of view, e.g. use of the new catering facility. Use of the indoor school, especially on match days – possibly exhibitions – possibly cinema shows for youngsters. Possibly setting up a children's playground for the very small, with responsible attendants. A centre for mothers to feed/change babies.

Sales items. Sales literature. Brand packaging, licensing.

Sponsorship/fund raising
Individuals responsible for geographical areas. Individuals responsible for sections of industry and commerce with incentives for those who obtain results. This team should be made up of professionals with contacts and experience.

Commercial enterprise team
This would probably include a representative from the holding company – fund raising – marketing/sales, the supporters supremo. To look into products from which the county could gain revenue, e.g. umbrellas, T-shirts, sweatshirts, car stickers, badges, supporters rosettes, ties, photographs, posters, raffles, aprons, scarves, plates, labels, beer mats, handbooks, past beneficiary brochures, calendars, videos, records, drawings, new cricket books – shop windows – special exhibitions – etc. This list is by no means comprehensive.

Cricket must be seen to take on the competition of other sports and leisure pursuits in an organised, determined, professional manner – decisions must be taken, and very soon. Delay through fear spells disaster.

There are many people involved in the game with knowledge and experience who would dearly love to work and help the county, but whose efforts have been shunned. They will *not* come back unless the county administrators ask and welcome them – never can it be said that there is nobody to help.

It is clear enough that help is needed. The increasing casualty rate amongst county secretaries in the early 1980s – five jobs changed hands in the 1982–83 close season alone – proves that the post of Chief Executive at a county club is becoming

increasingly harassing. Stanley Allen, senior partner of a respected firm of solicitors in Hove and a lifelong cricket-lover,
took on the job at Sussex in 1976. He soon realised the
demands of the multifarious duties involved, as the following
extract from an article he wrote for *The Cricketer* in 1983
would bear out:

'First and foremost the administration of a county
cricket club has increased enormously, particularly in
the last eight or nine years. There are several reasons.
Twenty years ago, in the heyday of the "retired-from-
the-services-type" secretary, there were no one-day
matches, no Sunday cricket, no sponsorship, no
requirement for massive fund raising, few overseas
player problems, far less paper-work (the TCCB
which, of necessity, produces a mass of paper-work,
was not even born). It was a comfortable job in those
far-off days for a comfortable person.

'Today's secretary must have the constitution of an
ox. He may find himself on duty in the summer for ten
days on the trot, including Sundays, and this will
include having to take the whole circus to a ground
away from his headquarters with all the hassle which
this includes. His home is no refuge. His telephone,
even though ex-directory, can ring at any time – day or
night – as committee members, players, members, the
media, seek his ear. Umpires, groundsmen, builders,
auditors, police, breweries, squash players, salesmen
of many wares, scorers, aspiring young cricketers,
undertakers wanting to scatter someone's ashes, the
TCCB, club doctor and physio – all need the secretary's time and attention.

'Yes, the job has changed out of all recognition, but
the old-fashioned members' club constitution remains,
and in my opinion (and this is not meant to be offensive
to my many friends who are members of county cricket
clubs) is a complete anachronism. Here is an example:

a county has an income of, say, £250,000. It is probable that less than one quarter of that will come from members' subscriptions. Yet under the present system in, I believe, all counties, the members have 100 per cent control, because it is they who elect vast committees on the basis of two or more members representing each of a number of districts in the county. The troubles of Yorkshire and the members' power struggles in that county illustrate my point.

'A county cricket club in 1983 is a complex business undertaking. It needs modern management and modern management disciplines and the committee system I have mentioned above is not only frustrating to all concerned, but is a hopeless method of government, ill-suited to such management – though in no way do I intend to denigrate the enormous amount of work which these committees attempt.

'Most counties need a massive injection of capital if they are to survive. It is a miracle that the seventeen have survived so far without one of the banks appointing a receiver. Sponsorship is a palliative; barring government subsidies (and why on earth not?) private capital must be sought. The flotation of Blankshire County Cricket Club Limited – paid up capital of £1,500 – surely cannot be long delayed. And those members zealous for the continuation of their county would, I am sure, be among the eager subscribers. The directors would, as in any company, be elected – and sacked – by their shareholders; a board of directors, five or seven, would decide the club's policy – and I mean *major* policy, such as the development and better use of the ground, captaincy, size of the playing staff, appointment of senior officers. A monthly board meeting in which the secretary (to give him his present day title) reported to the board and discussed policy matters seems like a dream for one who had to endure countless committees and sub-committees, very often overlapping one another's powers.

'When the revolution comes, the secretary should be given a free rein to run the show on the lines that the board have directed him. The members, many of whom would be shareholders in the company instead of paying subscriptions, could become season ticket holders in various grades. Why not?'

Of all the difficult moments in his few years at the helm in Hove, Allen recalls above all not such things as the bitter arguments at Lord's over Tony Greig's involvement in the Packer recruitments, but an incident of comedy and pathos one winter's morning. An elderly lady arrived with the ashes of her late husband, and asked for them to be scattered on the outfield of the county ground. As he was giving her a cup of tea in his office after the moving little ceremony, Stanley noticed to his horror that the groundsman's dog was busily engaged in digging away at the hallowed spot where the ashes had been laid to rest only a few minutes earlier!

This is not, one hopes, a symbolic story. But where does county cricket go from here? There is a growing feeling that if the Championship is to be continued, either one of the one-day competitions will have to be scrapped, or the uneconomic Championship itself will have to be reduced to fewer matches, probably played over four days to ensure as good preparation for Test cricket as possible.

There is something to be said for a two-divisional Championship, which would give some meaning to many games in the second half of the season which at present have little. The Championship, in whatever form it is played, needs to be regarded by all, not least the players, as the competition it is most important to win. This means also making it by far the most monetarily rewarding, although the prolonged search by the TCCB to find a new sponsor to succeed Schweppes after 1983 hardly bodes well for the future. (Britannic Assurance eventually took on the sponsorship for a minimum of three years.)

Suggestions have been made to involve the touring team in the Championship in some way, in order to restore more of the old 'bite' and sense of occasion to games which once were highlights of a county season. At the moment touring teams tend to use these games as practice for the Tests, while counties use them to rest senior players and try out young ones. If such a new scheme was practical – which, alas, is doubtful – points gained against the touring team could count towards the Championship, with additional prize money at stake for both touring side and county team. When generous prizes were offered by a sponsor in the late 1970s for such games, the problem was that the players still did not take the games as seriously as inter-county matches: so much for the belief that money is their only guiding principle. Moreover, since touring teams no longer play all the counties, the idea of awarding Championship points would raise new anomalies and bring back the days when percentage calculations determined Championship winners.

Another popular proposal is that one or more of the stronger Minor Counties, plus perhaps Ireland and Scotland, should join the Championship rather than lose their most talented players to first-class clubs.

The rub, as always, is money – which seems to shape every decision now made in professional cricket everywhere.

For all its problems, county cricket continued to be fun to follow in the press, usually fun to play, and frequently fun to watch in the two decades which followed the momentous decisions of 1963.

As we observed earlier, new competitions and overseas players allowed every one of the seventeen counties to harbour aspirations of glory. Nor did any one of them go through those twenty years without at least one major trophy to reward them for their efforts.

Derbyshire won the first NatWest Trophy with a scrambled single off the last ball of the match. Essex, who had won nothing in 102 years up to 1978, have since won the Championship twice, as well as the Benson and Hedges Cup and the John Player League. Glamorgan won their second Championship in 1969 and reached a Gillette final in 1977. Gloucestershire – so inspired by Mike Procter that they were known as Proctershire – won the Gillette in 1973 and the Benson and Hedges four years later. Hampshire have never won a major knockout competition, nor even reached a final at Lord's, but between 1973 and 1978 they won two John Player League titles and the Championship; they would, with normal luck, probably have won the Championship twice in successive years, had not five days in their last three matches in their 1974 campaign been completely washed out after they had led the table for most of the season. With Barry Richards and Gordon Greenidge opening the batting together at that time and Andy Roberts taking the new ball for them between 1974 and 1978, they were a formidable team, shrewdly led by Richard Gilliat. Now, under Nick Pocock's equally genial and determined captaincy, Hampshire promise almost as much in the mid-1980s, with Malcolm Marshall playing the Roberts role with equal effect and even greater tenacity.

Kent, with an almost entirely home-grown team, looked another side likely to prosper in the 1980s. They had successfully rebuilt after many days of triumph in the previous decade. They won or shared the Championship, the John Player and the Benson and Hedges competition three times each and, for good measure, added a Gillette Cup as well, having won this trophy for the first time in 1967. Between 1970 and 1978, in fact, they won ten titles, a record approached by no one else. In Kent's case, though Alan Knott, Derek Underwood and Asif Iqbal were outstanding, and Mike Denness was an underestimated captain, their success was largely a question of teamwork.

Lancashire's star has faded since they won the John Player in 1969 and 1970 and the Gillette four times in six years between 1970 and 1975. With Clive Lloyd to the fore, they were one of the first teams to cash in on the fashion for limited-overs cricket. The Manchester public supported the county in vast numbers when things were going well but they have proved fickle. Consequently the search for success at Old Trafford, which has included the appointment as manager of their former captain, Jack Bond, has recently been almost as feverish as it has been on the other side of the Pennines.

Leicestershire were another county to break their duck because of the greater opportunities afforded by overseas imports – not that they were anything new to this particular county – and by limited-overs cricket. Under Ray Illingworth they won the Benson and Hedges Cup in 1972 and 1975, the John Player League in 1974 and 1977, and the Championship in 1975.

England's other great post-war captain, Mike Brearley, shared in a number of triumphs with Middlesex. County champions in 1976, 1980 and 1982, they were also winners of the Gillette in 1977 and 1980 and the Benson and Hedges, under Mike Gatting, in 1983. The great strength of the county in these years was in bowling: Wayne Daniel from Barbados spearheaded the attack, but the English spinners, John Emburey and Phil Edmonds, often proved the match-winners in the fourth innings.

Northamptonshire, Somerset and Sussex were still without a win in the Championship when the 1984 season began, but all had their one-day triumphs – Sussex especially in the Gillette Cup, which they won under Ted Dexter in its first two years. Northants won the Gillette in 1976 and the Benson and Hedges four years later. Somerset, with three great individual cricketers who would have found their way into most imaginary world elevens between 1979 and 1983 – Viv Richards, Ian Botham and Joel Garner – won five limited-overs titles in those five years.

Nottinghamshire and Surrey, two of the great counties of the nineteenth century, took a long time to come to terms with the new era of opportunity and equality. Notts won the Championship in 1981, due largely to the fast bowling of Clive Rice from South Africa and Richard Hadlee from New Zealand. Surrey, after winning a solitary Championship in 1971, took the Benson and Hedges in 1974 but lost three Lord's finals in successive years before adding the NatWest Trophy to their many laurels in 1982.

Warwickshire, the wealthiest county by far as a result of the highly successful Supporters Association started in the 1950s by David Blakemore and his wife Winnie, have a magnificent modern headquarters at Edgbaston and the playing staff have always been well cared for. Leslie Deakins, an outstanding county secretary, made the most of these superb facilities funded by the Supporters Association largely from football pools. On the field the county has been generally a happy side – particularly so in recent years, when David Brown as manager and Bob Willis as captain have formed a professional but always cheerful partnership. Under the present secretary, A. C. Smith, Warwickshire won the Championship in 1972. In the 1960s they made three appearances in the Gillette Cup final, winning two of them under M. J. K. Smith and his namesake and successor, A.C. The Willis/Brown partnership has presided over some uneven performances but another trophy, the John Player, came in 1980.

Worcestershire have never been so strong or so buoyant in every way as they were in their Championship-winning seasons of 1964 and 1965, when Don Kenyon led a team greatly strengthened by the acquisition of Tom Graveney from Gloucestershire and Basil D'Oliveira from Cape Town. The fast bowling partnership of Jack Flavell and Len Coldwell was also crucial to the successes of that period. The long-serving left-arm spinner, Norman Gifford, took over the captaincy between 1971 and 1980 and in 1974 his team pinched the county title from Hampshire with a spirited late run. Worcestershire also won the John Player League in 1971 but in four appearances in a Lord's final they have been beaten each time.

The saddest county club in recent times has been the proudest and most successful of them all, Yorkshire. Two major reasons seem to account for their lack of success, in spite of the greater number of prizes available. First, the brave and worthy insistence on allowing only those men who have been born in Yorkshire to represent the county, put them at an immediate disadvantage when other counties were able to play world-class players from overseas. From 1979 only two players not qualified for England were allowed to play in any county match and in 1982 this was reduced to one per county, but by now a good many of the original imports had been in England long enough to become registered as home players. The other reason was a civil war of increasing bitterness, which has split both the players and the supporters of Yorkshire. At issue was the treatment of the third of the great Yorkshire opening batsmen to make a hundred hundreds, Geoffrey Boycott. At the end of the 1983 season – when Yorkshire finished bottom of the Championship for the first time, though they also won the John Player League for the first – he was sacked, despite scoring only a few under 2000 Championship runs and generally batting as well as ever in his forty-third year. This led to a revolution within the club. At a special general meeting the committee was defeated on a 'no confidence' motion, and Boycott was later reinstated as a player.

Yorkshire's dressing-room had been an unhappy place since the unwise sacking of Brian Close in 1970. In eight years under Boycott the county was nothing and the return of Ray Illingworth as manager – and, in 1982 and 1983, as manager-captain – was not the panacea so fervently sought. It was Illingworth's view that Boycott had become too big for the club, and certainly a thoroughly unhealthy personality cult had grown around him from the moment that, to his bitter resentment, he lost the captaincy. To outsiders the long, bitter civil war which followed was sad; for proud Yorkshire members it was demeaning and unworthy.

FOUR

Kerry Packer's Legacy

Kerry Packer will probably be remembered by most cricketers less for his personal battle to gain television rights in Australia than for raising the wages of leading professional players and introducing cricket by night. I believe I was the first to use the expression 'pyjama cricket' in a BBC report in 1978, when I tried to sum up my early reactions to night cricket in Australia. There was and is no doubt that floodlit cricket played in a warm climate is an exciting experience and a thrilling spectacle. But I loathed then, and still do, the razzmatazz which went with it. Coloured clothes were the visible symbol of Mr Packer's new, commercial cricket and they became, too, the symbol of the aggressive, 'liberated' player. By wearing them, Australia's top cricketers – and the many players from West Indies, England, South Africa and Pakistan who also signed secret and lucrative contracts to play unofficial cricket, in opposition to official Test matches during 1977 – were saying, it seemed, 'To hell with dignity and tradition. Pay us enough and we will wear anything or, if you wish, nothing.'

Night cricket was a brilliant idea and an obvious one, when you come to think of it, for any hot country. Provided it was not overdone, the cricket itself, even, I suppose, the white ball and the black sightscreen, were all acceptable. But to me the coloured clothes were not. The combination of Sydney's green grass and the matching green of the pavilion etched against a dark sky was impressive enough under floodlights without the unnecessary artificiality of coloured clothes and pads. The umpires, dressed in orange or mafia black, looked like fellow conspirators with the players. The whole thing was reminiscent of American baseball rather than cricket. Moreover, the general 'hype' for night cricket and the emphasis in the publicity for the night games on Australian nationalism tended to make one suspicious of the genuine competitiveness of the matches. 'Circus' was, at first, a not inappropriate term.

Many such gut reactions from the lover of traditional cricket may have been exaggerated. In one way they were irrational because as late as the second half of the nineteenth century coloured shirts were the accepted cricket dress in England: the All England XI of William Clarke, for example, wore white shirts with pink spots. Yet it was not easy to be objective at the time. Kerry Packer had overturned the established order of things.

Let us first be clear about his motives. He may well have been convinced that the Australian players were getting a bad deal: witness the often-quoted wide disparity in earnings between the golfer, Graham Marsh, and his more famous but infinitely less well rewarded, monetarily speaking, brother, Rodney. But Packer's prime intention, having been refused the right to televise Test cricket in Australia (which was riding high on the crest of the Lillee/Thomson/Chappell wave), despite offering more money than the Australian Broadcasting Commission, was to bulldoze his way past the Australian Cricket Board's barriers and get his own way by force.

Cleverly, he exploited the fact that top-class cricketers – notably in Australia, but also in the other Test-playing countries – were earning minimal direct rewards from playing matches which attracted many thousands of spectators and generated large revenues. This money had traditionally been ploughed back into the game, but already international cricket was starting to be played more frequently, giving greater problems for those who tried to play it on a semi-amateur basis whilst holding down another job. Once a few of the senior Australian players (some of whom, like Ian Chappell and Dennis Lillee, perhaps inclined by nature to be rebellious) had accepted the generous wages Packer offered in order to set up matches in rivalry with the ACB, most of the rest of the world's best cricketers followed. When you are being offered a very large sum of money, it is easy enough to convince yourself that the money is not the only motive for casting aside loyalty to anyone else. In the case of the Australians the loyalty to their cricket board was not very strong anyway. The same was true of the West Indians and Pakistanis, who made up the bulk of the rest of the players who formed 'World Series Cricket', as the Packer circus became known once it began to demand serious attention as well as angry derision. For the English players there was perhaps less excuse, because first-class cricketers had for many years been well represented in the higher councils of the game. But it is not difficult to understand why most of them went, especially those for whom Test cricket had lost its novelty and allure, or who felt insecure about their position at the top and were suddenly offered a large sum of money for a short-term contract. For all of them, too, there was the thrill of a pioneering effort and the feeling that they were fighting to improve the lot of their fellow professionals.

'There is something of the whore in all of us,' Mr Packer had said very early in the saga, 'and everyone has his price.' He then proceeded to prove the truth of his statement.

For two seasons World Series Cricket was promoted in opposition to the traditional fare of an Australian season: Sheffield Shield matches and Test cricket. At first, the establishment withstood the revolution, relying on the innate conservatism of most cricket spectators and on restrictive contracts to keep the remaining players in their own employ. In England, the Cornhill sponsorship of Test matches was conjured up out of the crisis, to the benefit of everyone – not least Cornhill. A small, relatively unknown insurance grouping, within a few years they became one of the big league. England's Test players and umpires, meanwhile, received a five hundred per cent pay rise almost overnight.

The Australian players had effectively had much less representation in the management of the game than their English counterparts. But, ironically, following the setting-up of a cricket committee of the ACB early in the 1976–77 season, they had been getting, in the words of Greg Chappell, 'dramatically increased rewards', even before the Packer contracts were offered. Agreements between the ACB and sponsors meant that a Test player who kept fit throughout the 1977 home and away seasons would have earned some £12,000. Four of the State captains who sat on the committee which helped to negotiate these sponsorship deals were, at the same time, secretly dealing with the Packer organisation. The subsequent fury of Australian administrators was understandable.

The quality of players might have been higher in WSC, but on the whole the Australian public preferred 'fair dinkum cricket' and so, significantly, did most of the cricket press. The 'fly boy' impression given by the public relations team used to promote the new form of cricket offended most of those with a feel for the game and its history. Clearly, their business was to make money out of cricket. Many of them thought it was a boring old game which needed jazzing up. They understood dollars better than off-drives.

For some time the old order held firm and it looked as though Mr Packer had backed an expensive loser: such were his reserves, he could afford to. Meanwhile his matches were played before largely empty houses. It was his lawyers rather than his players who helped him turn the tide, by successfully challenging the ban on his players from other cricket competitions in the High Court of England and by winning the right to play on Australia's most famous ground, the Sydney Cricket Ground. Here floodlights were erected – great, ugly, 200-foot-high concrete towers, which dwarfed the old Edwardian stands – and the young of Sydney came to see the new form of cricket, attracted by a massive publicity campaign on Packer's own television channel.

This triumph had been preceded by a clear defeat in the war of winning customers engendered by a successful Test series between India, under Bishen Bedi, and the Australian 'second eleven'. The Indians relied mainly on spinners who, being slow, were classified as 'boring' by some of the commercial men in the Packer organisation. World Series Cricket, in contrast, offered 'blood and thunder', sometimes genuine, sometimes contrived. When it was genuine it led to much ferocious fast bowling, largely unchecked by umpires. For most batsmen, the helmet became sensible protection.

The success of the Australia versus India series in 1977–78 was followed by England's five-one victory in the Ashes series the following year. This was a disaster for the Australian Cricket Board. Australian crowds have always tended to be smaller when their national side is losing and this time gates declined dramatically – more than fifty per cent fewer people watched the six Tests of 1978–79 than had massed to see Lillee and Thomson 'knocking off the Poms' in 1974–75. Had Australia done better the ACB might have sweated the contest out longer. As it was, they were driven to the conference table and an agreement was reached which gave them back their ostensible control of the cricket programme in Australia whilst for ten years Packer's company, Publishing and Broadcasting Pty Ltd (PBL), was granted sole rights to the promotion of cricket in Australia.

The agreement was made on 30 May 1979, two years after the first incredible announcement of the defections of, initially, thirty-five cricketers. Both sides had been ready for compromise, the Board because of the poor financial results of the Ashes series and their desire to get back their top players at almost any price, and the Packer camp because, despite achieving increased credibility and success in their second season of operation (and in particular one night of triumph when, it was claimed, 50,000 people watched the first of the night games at the SCG), the enterprise overall had lost in excess of £1,500,000. The estimate of WSC's managing director, Andrew Caro, in his book *With a Straight Bat* was 'over 3,000,000 dollars'. Overheads, including all the heavy wage packets and the hiring of large grounds, had outweighed income from advertising and gate receipts. Every means of marketing had been used – radio, press and, above all, Channel Nine television. Nor had any expense been spared on the television coverage itself; an army of cameramen and commentators produced a steadily improving technical portrayal of each match, using graphics to explain to the uninitiated such things as bouncers and yorkers.

The two-year experience of WSC gave the marketing men of PBL valuable experience when it came to selling cricket once Mr Packer had forced his way past the official door and, effectively, into the chair of the Australian Cricket Board. Packer himself, it is true, did not want that chair – he moved on to other things – but his employees have remained powerful in the decisions made about Australian cricket since the truce in 1979.

The players, originally the willing pawns in a war about television rights were, in a monetary sense at least, the other winners of the whole unpleasant affair. Having once had only a modest but enjoyable life style against a background of insecurity, first-class cricketers who reached the top after 1976 became big money earners. Below Test level, players of more modest ability have also tended to do better, partly as a result of the greater awareness amongst cricket administrators of the commercial possibilities of cricket. But, at least in England, the industrial market had already been tapped by cricket and there are signs, five years on, that it is a strictly limited one. Throughout the 1983 cricket season, for example, the Test and County Cricket Board were searching frantically for a successor to the Prudential, who felt that they had got all they could out of linking their name with one-day internationals and the World Cup, and also to Schweppes, who had decided to pull out of their sponsorship of the County Championship. Eventually Texaco took on the first patronage and, as already mentioned, Britannic Assurance the other one.

In Australia the most enduring WSC achievement was night cricket under floodlights. Another successful experiment, though, was completed in the first year by the future Perth groundsman, John Maley: he created grass wickets of excellent quality in a greenhouse and then had them dropped by cranes into the middle of football grounds. This was a brilliant idea, but also an ambitious one, especially as perfectly good artificial grass wickets already existed. It showed how concerned the WSC players were to prove the genuineness of their cricket. But to the true followers of the game such wickets never became acceptable. One of the many lessons of WSC was that cricket cannot be separated from its history and traditions.

Another enduring legacy of 'Packer cricket' was the idea of 'circles' in one-day matches, inside which a certain number of players had to field at certain times. Though it was an artificiality, it certainly helped to make field-placing less defensive.

On the debit side of the affair, let there be no doubt that the instigators of WSC were parasites, using players they had done nothing to develop and giving precious little back to cricket in return. The split in the game caused deep and sad disagreements, often amongst old friends. Following the High Court judgement of Mr Justice Slade in November 1979, effectively allowing players to serve two masters, the game has tended to become obsessed with the subject of money and for a time there was a danger that winning would become so important that cheating would be resorted to if necessary. Incredibly, a batsman was given out in a Test between Australia and Pakistan for picking up the ball and handing it to the bowler. Happily though, both players and umpires between them have reacted instinctively against a decline to these sort of standards. There will be more to say later about player power, but since the Packer revolution was originally about television it is worth pointing out here that now that the eye of television scrutinises every move by the players in almost every big match, it has become all the more important for them to play the game responsibly.

In Australia it has needed official 'codes of conduct' to try to ensure that this happens but the code has been pusillanimously enforced. In England, the tradition of tough but chivalrous rivalry in the County Championship happily makes such written rules unnecessary. As the French Revolution could never have occurred in England because of the greater flexibility of British society, so the Packer revolution could never have begun in England because of the camaraderie of county cricket.

Even in England, however, there have been signs of 'corruption'. It has become commonplace for counties to prepare their home pitches to suit their own bowlers – Nottinghamshire in 1981 were not alone in doing so. In addition county delegates at TCCB meetings have voted for reasons of self-interest rather than the common good on such issues as the number of overseas players. These are symptoms of the same commercial attitude engendered by Packer.

FIVE

After the Revolution
Commercial Corruption in Modern Australian Cricket

It took a long, long time for the wounds opened up by Packer to heal. In some ways, in fact, cricket will always bear the scars. Whether Australian cricket is healthier now than it was in 1976 is questionable. Certainly it is radically changed.

Certainly, too, the revolution enabled Australia to be the pioneer of commercial cricket. Other countries may disapprove of some of the rapid changes which have been made, but they must also admit that many of the ideas now pursued in harness by PBL and the Australian Cricket Board have proved successful. In this sense at any rate, if not in all senses, Australia has taken over from England – once embodied as MCC – as the leader of world cricket.

It was not until the England tour of 1982–83 that the Australian authorities worked out a programme which made sense both from a player's and an administrator's point of view. Until then the obsession with one-day cricket threatened to swamp not only the Sheffield Shield but also Test cricket. PBL publicity tended to be aimed almost exclusively at getting the crowds in to watch the one-day internationals, and very successful it was too. In 1981–82, crowds attracted by the West Indies for one-day internationals included gates of 52,053 at Sydney, 22,608 at Brisbane (where the largest crowd since the modernisation of the Gabba had been only 18,579 for a single day of a Test), 26,446 at Perth, and 78,147 at the Melbourne Cricket Ground. An even bigger crowd, 86,133, saw Australia v West Indies in 1983–84 – at Melbourne again, of course.

One cannot argue with figures like these. Bottoms on seats

mean beyond any doubt that the cricket being provided is attractive. Yet anyone with a feel for cricket began to get heartily sick of seeing West Indies, Australia and Pakistan playing each other over and over again in matches of the same type, with the same players pursuing the same tactics in matches often following a course easily predictable after the first twenty overs. These three teams played nineteen one-day internationals (and six Tests) in 1981–82, and another seventeen internationals two years later.

It was in the first of these years that Lynton Taylor, the industrious, thorough, experienced and in many ways enlightened managing director of PBL, made an extraordinary statement – to the effect that he feared for the future of Test cricket unless its character were to be altered. He described Test cricket as 'archaic' (this, of course, it is, which is one of the reasons for its attraction) and added: 'I do not know that it can be saved. I hope so but I am not convinced. People will no longer sit through five days of a match. Those days are long gone. People don't go to watch beautiful defensive shots or the battle of tactics any more. Unless something is done to change the rules and the manner in which it is played, then officials will have a hard time to make it attractive.'

This really was an incredible statement which one likes to think he may now regret. To be fair to Mr Taylor, it was made soon after the Australia versus Pakistan Test at Melbourne had attracted a mere 33,768 people over five days, this on the ground which once (against West Indies in 1960–61) held 90,800 spectators for a single day's Test cricket. At about this time England were playing India in Calcutta in a sterile series, yet an estimated 394,000 attended the five days of the match. Moreover, part of the reason for the poor crowds at the Tests against Pakistan was that the latter were being unfavourably compared by the Australian public with the West Indies. Given a choice of seeing one or the other, most people settled for Clive Lloyd's team rather than Javed Miandad's. And if they had the choice of seeing them in a Test or in one of the nineteen one-day internationals played in that 1981–82 season alone, many preferred the guarantee of batsmen on the attack and a result in one day. In other words, the over-full programme of international cricket, so proudly marketed by PBL, was one of the main reasons for the poor gate at that particular match.

Fortunately the Australia versus West Indies Test series that season, though it was confusingly mixed in with the one-day internationals, did grip the public imagination, especially because Australia managed to win the First Test, draw the Second and thus go into the Third at Adelaide one up. This time the West Indies won a thrilling contest, after which Kim Hughes, the Australian vice-captain, made a characteristically ingenuous statement: 'We got a bigger thrill out of beating the West Indies in the Sydney Test than ever we could out of winning a one-day competition.' This was not the sort of honest appraisal which players had been making in the early days after the schism. The line until now had been, it seemed, 'pay us enough and we'll play under any rules all day and all night'.

But, to their credit, Lynton Taylor's PBL team and the ACB began to accept criticisms (from interfering diehards like myself!) that they were over-selling one-day cricket and under-selling the traditional Test match. They were also forced to take notice of two highly critical statements by the managers of the West Indian and Pakistani tours in 1981–82. Ijaz Butt observed that 'chopping and changing all over a big country like Australia just does not do any good for a player's ability to produce his best . . . players will soon start objecting to being treated as financial bait and want to be treated as human beings.'

Here was an uncomfortable echo, if the players of Australia had any consciences, of exactly what they had been complaining about pre-Packer. Hughes confirmed as much: 'The amount of cricket we are playing is taking its toll . . . The enjoyment we get from the game is being severely tested.'

Perhaps this is inevitable when amateurs become professionals, but the point was that the programme the new professionals were being asked to play in was both tiring and monotonous. As the West Indian manager, Steve Camacho, observed: 'For the benefit of Australian cricket a better balance must be found. With the best players playing one one-day match after another and seldom being seen in the Sheffield Shield, the quality of cricket is bound to drop.' Most of us came to exactly this conclusion after Brearley's second tour as captain in 1979–80. In that season Hughes remained perfectly fit throughout but, because of international commitments, he was unable to play for Western Australia in a single Shield game.

By the time England returned, in 1982–83, the message had finally begun to sink in. Against their will, it seems, PBL agreed to the TCCB's wish (by now supported by the ACB and the Australian players) to play the Test matches as an entity in themselves, leaving the 'feast' of one-day internationals (cut to seventeen this time) until the New Year, when the series for the Ashes was over. Apparently PBL feared that the Tests would dissuade people from going to watch the limited-overs games. But they went to work on selling the Test series with a vigour and imagination they had not shown since the days of World Series Cricket. Emotions were stirred by film commercials showing 'typical Poms' making complacent statements about the Aussies being no good and England being bound to win the Ashes. Whether this propaganda was desirable or really necessary to 'sell' Tests which had always attracted huge crowds in Australia is very doubtful. The fact is, however, that over half a million people (538,601) went to the five Tests and a further 551,465 then turned up for the triangular one-day series between Australia, England and New Zealand. Thus the magic million was comfortably passed, with plentiful spin-off profits for PBL and the ACB from 'cricketing merchandise' and, of course, big advertising revenue for Channel Nine during their extensive, brash and popular television coverage.

It is not merely being cynical to observe, however, that their big crowds were attracted partly because of the fact that the Australian team was being successful. Australia won the Ashes series two–one and eventually carried off the one-day trophy too. Support would undoubtedly have been less impressive if Australia had played in 1982–83 as they did in England a few months later when the nadir of a dismal World Cup campaign was a defeat by Zimbabwe, a team of talented, but part-time, cricketers. Not for the first time the touring team in England failed to play with the harmony and discipline necessary for consistent success. A long-running dispute between Hughes, the captain, and Lillee, his illustrious but controversial fast bowler, was never far from the surface.

This was another legacy from the Packer schism, during which Hughes had been, as it were, on the side of the angels. Hughes became captain of Western Australia against the wishes of that State's two senior players, Lillee and Rodney Marsh. Though neither, so far as I have ever seen at any rate, ever gave less than his best when playing under Hughes, both made it plain that they would rather be playing under someone else. With such an attitude from his senior players, how could Hughes gain confidence in himself? Whenever Greg Chappell, brother of an Australian captain loved by his own players but disapproved of for his open defiance of the conventions of cricket by a great many Australians, was available to lead his country, Hughes was always demoted to the vice-captaincy. Moreover, he tended to take on the purple when the Empire was most under threat. He it was who led Australia away from home in Pakistan, India and England. Apart from one short tour of Pakistan, Greg Chappell (who, incidentally, had been clapped all the way to the pavilion after his last innings of the 1977 series in England having announced his retirement!) preferred to stay at home and tend his family and business interests. You could take one of two views about this. Either that Chappell, Australia's finest contemporary batsman, who had done his bit in the way of overseas touring in his youth, had every right now to pick and choose where and when he played and, moreover, that he must take his chance on whether or not the selectors asked him to be captain when he played; or that he had a right to choose when he was available but he could not expect under these circumstances to be considered for the captaincy. The selectors took the former view, and so it was that Chappell at last led Australia to victory in an Ashes series in 1982–83. He retired, after one more successful season a year later, with more Test runs than anyone for Australia, and more Test catches than anyone in any country. Two more record-breakers, Dennis Lillee and Rodney Marsh, followed him into retirement, tired but prosperous.

This long-running captaincy saga might have been averted had the Australian Board turned instead to a man who had the character and natural authority to stand above the petty passions of the Packer upheaval. John Inverarity has led West Australia to success in the Sheffield Shield on four occasions. Until then, the Sandgropers, as they are picturesquely known, had never won the Shield. Inverarity, still playing cricket in 1983–84, though now in South Australia as deputy-headmaster of a large private school, would have had the tactical skill, authority and respect needed to bring the best out of Lillee, Marsh and Hughes, as well as the ability just about to hold his own as a player in his own right (as Brearley just managed to do for England, his captaincy being worth an incalculable number of runs and wickets) and the grace to restore the dignity of Australian cricket.

Although Kim Hughes, confirmed as captain in 1983–84, has seldom put a foot wrong in a diplomatic sense, he does not have the stature of Inverarity. Greg Chappell, on the whole, does, but being not far from the van of the Packer revolution, he was too much a part of the brash commercialism of modern Australian cricket to be able to stand apart from it. In any case, his image as a dignified leader was deeply dented by a notorious decision – to tell his brother, Trevor, to bowl an underarm 'sneak' when New Zealand needed six to win off the last ball of a one-day international. That this one incident should have caused an international furore, with public comments made by the prime ministers of both Australia and New Zealand, was evidence that the convention of chivalry in cricket was not yet a mere myth, nor an invention of cricket historians. People still cared about sportsmanship in cricket, Australians included.

But those in authority no longer seem prepared to do anything about it. There was another, less publicised incident during New Zealand's tour that same season (1981–82) when Chappell was, in the eyes of the vast majority, clearly caught by Martin Snedden in the deep. The umpires were apparently watching for possible run-outs and when Chappell refused to walk they felt unable to give him out. Yet a television view clearly proved the catch to be legal. This was one time, surely, when the camera could sensibly and legitimately have been used by the umpires to ensure justice. But that is a topic for later discussion; the point here is that the Australian captain appeared to be prepared to win at all costs.

This is not to say that Chappell is any more ruthless than many other Test cricketers, from W.G. onwards. But this kind of incident, along with Lillee's escape from any proper punishment – for such deeds as throwing his aluminium bat across the field in public protest in the middle of a Test match he had already held up for several minutes whilst arguing with the umpires; kicking an opponent, Javed Miandad, in another Test; and betting against his own team at Headingley in 1981, then denying he had done so officially only to reveal months later in a book that the denial was false – suggest that Australian cricket has sold its soul to commerce.

It has apparently become less important to most of those involved in the marketing and administration of Australian cricket to defend the dignity of the game than to boost its profits. To have banned Lillee from Test cricket for any or all of his misdemeanours would have been not only to deprive Australia of its best fast bowler but also of its greatest draw-card. People want to watch Lillee, and since the public pay their wishes must be paramount. This is not, perhaps, a fair reflection of the motives of the Australian Cricket Board in disciplinary matters, but it is undoubtedly one essential consideration. Any decision has to be made, consciously or unconsciously, with regard to its effect on gate money and advertising revenue.

The control exercised by Channel Nine television sometimes goes beyond the marketing of the game. There was indisputable evidence of this during England and New Zealand's triangular one-day series with Australia in 1982–83. Officially, four minutes were allowed for each over (with television commercials, of course, between) but on two occasions when rain stopped play in the middle of a match, far more overs were taken off than was necessary. In an England versus Australia match, the match was reduced by twenty-six overs for a stoppage of only an hour, while in an Australia versus New Zealand match twelve overs were deducted for a twenty-minute break. Thus television schedules were protected from the possibility of the game finishing after peak viewing time. More sinister still, it was pointed out by some observers that Australia were batting second on both occasions. By having the number of overs – and their own winning target – greatly reduced, Australia's chances of victory were correspondingly enhanced. No umpire would ever be party to any witting manipulation on behalf of the home side, or of any side, and it may have been pure chance that Australia happened to have the advantage of batting second on these occasions – but PBL have never made any secret of the importance to them of having Australia in the finals. The previous year, indeed, Australia appeared doomed to take the wooden spoon, but a remarkable run of late victories demoted Pakistan at the last gasp and ensured that Australia would play West Indies in the final. Then, in 1984, the West Indies were obliged to play a third final, having won the first and 'tied' the second, despite losing fewer wickets than Australia.

I would not accuse anyone of deliberate collusion or home-town bias. But it is clear enough that with television having either at first hand, through Channel Nine, or at second through its brother-company, PBL, so firm a say in the conduct of Australian commercial cricket, the temptation must sometimes be great. From the players' point of view, winning any

Test or international nowadays in any country is no longer just a matter of prestige, patriotism and honour. By winning the Benson and Hedges one-day trophy in 1983–84, for example, the West Indies team earned themselves a total of £56,000. Not surprising, therefore, that those who disapprove of playing in coloured clothes – such as the shocking pink the West Indians had to wear in the first of the post-Packer triangular tournaments – are happy nevertheless to obey the dictates of the television producers, who believe coloured clothes mean colourful cricket. Equally, the rest day in the middle of a Test, a long-established and in my view necessary break, has been sacrificed in order to pack more international cricket into the Australian season.

So long as there are cricketing reasons for changes of this nature, or provided that changes made for commercial reasons do not seriously affect the character of the cricket played, then clearly there is good reason for those who have the skill to exploit the commercial possibilities of cricket to have their way, within reason. The massive television exposure of top-class cricketers and the tendency for the marketing men to build relatively ordinary players into 'superstars' may not be good for the cricket – though it is for the bank balances – of the players concerned. To give but one example, David Hookes would have achieved more than he has had he not been elevated to superstar status by World Series Cricket looking for a young, blond Australian batting hero. Brilliant batsman as he is, he would have profited from less exploitation of his talents off the field and more hard work in fostering them on it. But the fact that Hookes is a hero for a generation of Australian youth is good for cricket. It is the responsibility of those promoting cricket to encourage people to play the game as well as to watch it. This, in turn, means inspiring the young. In this respect at least, my impression is that Australian cricket is currently very healthy.

Where, speaking in general terms, the players and the promoters have jointly failed, is in maintaining the right image for cricket. Once one associated Australian cricket with such enduring qualities as courage, enterprise, determination to win and genuine sportsmanship. Now, alas, because the bad boys have been glorified, the image, though in the majority of cases it is unfair, tends to be one of uncouth arrogance. This is tragic both for cricket and for Australia, whose less desirable youth element has thus been attracted, especially by one-day cricket at night, and who could sour the game in the same way that British soccer hooligans have soured football.

Those spectators, moreover, appear to have little interest in Australian domestic cricket at first-class level. The one-day knockout cup between the State teams, the Macdonalds Cup, has not attracted the same sort of enthusiasm and support as the Gillette Cup did in England after 1963. It would be a major surprise if in England either the NatWest or the Benson and Hedges finals failed to attract a full house at Lord's. But big crowds for State matches in Australia are, it seems, a thing of the past and those for the traditional competition, the Sheffield Shield, have in recent years sunk, proportionately at least, even lower than for the County Championship. In October 1982, during a Shield match between New South Wales and Tasmania, the Sydney Cricket Ground Trust (which owns the ground) and the New South Wales Cricket Association decided to close the ground's most famous landmark – and for the casual public its most popular area – the Hill. In order to cut the cost of staging the match still further, the information normally given on the huge scoreboard at the back of the Hill was reduced to a bare minimum because fewer hands were paid to operate it. In 1984 the old scoreboard came down and a new electronic one took its place.

To an even greater degree than in England, Australian cricket has become completely dependent on the income from international and Test cricket. Yet performances for State teams remain the only way for players to catch the eyes of the selectors and thus bid for their share of the prizes available at the top. But the gap between the rest and those who eventually win those prizes and become wealthy, like Marsh, Lillee or Hookes (who was paid $A5000 in 1982 by one company simply to grow a beard and then have it shaved off in public by a couple of models), is an even bigger one than in other sports. Whereas Hookes is seen as a commercial hot property, young Dirk Wellham, despite scoring a century in his first Test match, against England at The Oval in 1981, is not. At that stage Wellham was a qualified schoolteacher but, not unnaturally after such a start, he decided to concentrate full-time on cricket. Within six months he lost his place in both the Test and State teams. Esso employed him on the strength of a single interview but saw him as a less valuable employee when his cricket career began to falter and in 1983 they sacked him on the grounds that they could hardly keep him on part-time when full-time staff were being asked to retire early at a time of generally high unemployment.

As Wellham pointed out: 'Shield players have to sacrifice as much time to cricket as Test players but receive only five per cent of the income.' The counter-argument is that it is the Test players, not the State players, who attract the big crowds and generate the income: but this is only half the story. The Test players would never have emerged but for their success in Shield cricket.

The problem is aggravated by the fact that, because the rewards at the top of Australian cricket have become so much greater since the Packer revolution, the leading players are staying in the game much longer. Thus there is no longer the swift turnover which kept Australian cricket so virile at international level during the first century of Test cricket. So there is less incentive for the young hopefuls and many, clearly, will be forced to give the game up unless profits from the big matches are used to bolster the salaries of Shield players, albeit artificially.

As for the Shield matches themselves, more sponsorship and promotion at State level seems essential. Australian cricket took an irrevocable step towards becoming a fully professional sport when, for better or worse, the ACB did their deal with Mr Packer.

SIX

Test Cricket
Too Much of a Good Thing

A would-be cricket promoter (of high repute) got in touch with me in 1983, asking how easy it would be to get all the leading all-rounders of world cricket, a particularly brilliant collection at the time, together for a tournament of champions. Sponsorship and television had, he said, been arranged. All that was necessary now was to find a time when it would be possible to get Ian Botham, Kapil Dev, Imran Khan, Richard Hadlee, Viv Richards and Greg Chappell together in the same place. Only two or three clear days were required, as modern transport would enable the promoter to whisk the players from whatever country they were in to the appropriate place.

It was a good idea of its kind. The trouble was that it proved impossible in the winter of 1983–84 to find even one day when one or more of the players was not engaged in playing for his country. This is not to say that if the money had been good enough most of them would not have found a reason for attending, but the episode was a powerful illustration of the hectic life of the modern international player and of the proliferation of international cricket which threatens to reach overkill proportions.

The problems faced by first-class cricket in the United Kingdom in the 1960s and 1970s were more or less reflected in all of the so-called 'developed' countries of the game. The solution which each country came to independently was to plan a home series of Test matches every season. In the last five years these Tests have been supplemented by an increasing number of one-day internationals. Indeed in Australia, as already observed, it became in the years after Packer a question of Tests supplementing one-day internationals. Either way, international cricket was steadily subordinating, and in danger of altogether submerging, all other first-class cricket.

The first 100 Test matches were played at a rate of three games a year, between 1877 and 1908. Those thirty-one years for the first 100 became twenty-three years for the next – subtracting, that is, the five years of the first world war in which no Test cricket, of course, was played. Either side of the second world war, between the Australia versus West Indies Test at Sydney in January 1931 and the England versus Australia Test at Lord's in 1948, another 100 Tests were played. In 1928 and 1930 respectively, West Indies and New Zealand had joined the pioneers, followed by India in 1932 (and Pakistan in 1954, Sri Lanka in 1982) thus adding greater variety but inevitably swelling the number of games. The real proliferation, though, came after the second world war and especially in the years after the Packer revolution when, in order to stop players signing for Packer or any other promoter, or going to play instead in South Africa, the Cricket Boards sought to keep their top players as occupied and well rewarded as possible. The 400th Test came in 1955, the 500th in 1961, the 600th in 1966, the 700th in 1972, the 800th in 1977 and the 900th in 1980–81. The 1000th Test match will be played this winter, 1984–85.

Regular Test cricketers can now expect to play in at least twelve Tests in a year. In fact England were scheduled to play no fewer than twenty-six Tests between January 1984 and August 1985. In eighteen months a regular player may thus pack in as many Tests – not to mention one-day internationals – as his counterpart of even thirty years back might have played in four or five years. And, though professional careers are inevitably shorter with so much high-pressure cricket, and bigger rewards, there are many more eighteen months in a career than there are five years!

To players and spectators alike the sense of a great occasion whenever a Test match begins has inevitably grown less keen. It would be wrong to say it has gone altogether. To me, the excitement of the first ball of any Test remains vivid; but to anyone not wholly devoted to the game there must be a feeling of 'not another Test between England and Australia – they only played each other in the other country a couple of months ago'. And that feeling is not far wrong. England, for example, played internationals against New Zealand in Australia in 1983, more internationals in New Zealand before they went home, more in England against the New Zealand touring team – two more meetings in the World Cup – plus a series of four Tests later in the same season. Then in the early days of January 1984 back they went to New Zealand for more Tests and one-day internationals. As it happened, the matches between the two teams were generally contested honourably and attractively, but really, what planning!

Between October 1983 and May 1984 there were twenty-eight Tests and thirty-nine one-day internationals played round the world between combinations of the seven Test-playing countries. Nor will it be long before Zimbabwe, who showed in the 1983 World Cup that they can hold their own in high company (they defeated Australia once and pushed them close a second time), join the fold.

As a result of all this increased international activity, records have become telescoped and in many cases mean less. Sunil Gavaskar, for example, equalled Sir Donald Bradman's number of Test hundreds – twenty-nine – in 1984 but it took him forty-three more Tests and over twice as many innings to reach the goal. Equally important, the increased exposure of cricketers afforded by television has removed the mystique once enjoyed by Test players who were known to followers only through articles, reports and photographs in newspapers and magazines, or by an occasional distant glimpse from the boundary's edge. Now we have their every grimace and smile in our sitting-rooms, as well as their cover-drives and diving catches. For every young watcher hooked as a result, others are probably being forced away from the game, familiarity having bred contempt. There are other hobbies and other sports and other things to watch. The steadily declining crowds for soccer are a warning to cricket of what overkill may do. There can always be too much of any good thing, and it is essential that the Test-playing countries should get together to agree a self-denying ordinance limiting them to, say, six home Tests and four one-day internationals per home season.

There was a time when England, knowing the wisdom of such a limitation, might have been able to impose it on the other members of the International Cricket Conference; what is more, the other nations would willingly have concurred. Now that Australian commercial interests have set the trend, however, it is impossible to imagine the Australian Board, for example, agreeing to any such limitation. In their case, therefore, recognising the undoubted popularity of limited-overs internationals there and the profits accruing, which benefit not just the Australians but the visiting countries too, a compromise figure of six Tests and a maximum of six internationals between any two countries (i.e. twelve games in a triangular tournament) might be acceptable and prevent further escalation.

Profit, of course, is what the whole argument is about. The players may feel in their hearts that they are playing too much Test cricket, but human nature precludes them from turning down any opportunity to share the rich rewards these games bring. Equally, administrators know the dangers of killing the golden goose, but they are tempted to make it lay as many eggs as possible in order to pay for all the less profitable cricket run under their auspices. But those other first-class competitions like the County Championship, the Ranji Trophy and the Sheffield Shield are demeaned if the leading players are not taking part. A summer without Tests, if ever it came again, would make a pleasant and interesting change.

And yet, of course, we would miss much. Much more often than not Test cricket still provides a wonderful spectacle. When players such as the all-rounders mentioned earlier are locked in chivalrous combat, it is inspiring to the young and invigorating to the rest of us. Attack has been the key to the attraction and success of Botham, Kapil Dev, Imran Khan and Hadlee alike. The bare-headed belligerence, in the age of helmets and safety-first tactics, of Botham at Headingley and Old Trafford in 1981, and of Kapil Dev throughout the Indian tour the following summer, matched the imperious hostility of Imran and the masterly control of Hadlee with the ball in series against Australia and England. Between them, these all-rounders plus Richards and Chappell, the supreme batsmen of the last decade, have shown that standards of international cricket can still be as high as in earlier periods. It is a different game, more aggressive, dominated by a greater number of fast bowlers and more ruthless than ever before, but it still produces its champions, its unexpected heroes, and its dramatic matches.

Apart from overkill, the most serious danger to the future of Test cricket in the last twenty years has come from the steady decline in work-rate in the field, a problem now tackled effectively in those countries where agreement has been reached by the two competing sides to play a minimum number of overs in a day. It was a tour by England to India of rare turgidity, even by the sluggish standards of the sub-continent, which led at last to action being taken to give the customers a bit more cricket for their money. In this 1981–82 series over-rates got down as low as thirteen an hour, the average rate by both sides in the Delhi Test. This was a game England needed to win, being one down in the series. India managed to slow things down to the same extent despite the fact that three spin bowlers delivered 76 of the 156.4 overs in England's first innings.

Slowing the game down had become a recognised and all too infrequently deplored tactic in first-class, but especially in Test, cricket since the infamous day at Melbourne in the New Year Test of 1955 when England under Len Hutton bowled only 54 eight-ball overs in five hours. There were mitigating circumstances in that the heat was desperately enervating, but the point was that the dilatoriness was tactical. Umpires then, and for ever after, have been unwilling to apply the Law stating quite clearly that any form of time-wasting is unfair. (The new Code of Laws made this all the clearer but, as far as I am aware, action has never been taken under Law 42 3, note 10.)

Fertilised outfields, allowing the shine to stay on the ball so that a pack of three or four fast bowlers may hunt together all day if necessary; balls with more prominent seams; taller and fitter fast bowlers; and more athletic fielding have all contributed to a marked drop in over-rates, and in runs scored during the day, in the last twenty years. The actual rate of runs scored per over has not changed significantly, but the following figures, produced for this book by statistician Idris Barrett, dramatically reveal the pattern of change.

The figures were produced according to the following guidelines:

1. Only drawn matches should be included because finished games would mean that not all the available time had been utilised.

2. Such matches should be free of any frequent or prolonged stoppages for rain.

3. Only matches in England with six-ball overs should be studied, thus excluding Tests before 1902 and the season of 1939.

4. Main spinners are normally easily enough categorised, but in the cases of Garfield Sobers and S. F. Barnes half of the overs of each were taken to be of spin, half of pace.

Apart from the staggering fact that only one of the games reviewed before 1953 had an average number of fewer than 300 runs in a day (Leeds, 1935) and not one after 1953 an average number higher than 270, the tables are a remarkable illustration of the truth of Parkinson's Law: work expands to fill the time available.

The following figures illustrate clearly that, as Test matches have increased their duration to five days, fewer overs have been bowled in a day's play. The Tests of three or four days

DRAWN MATCHES IN ENGLAND

Season	Ground	England's opponents	Days of play	Total runs scored	Wkts down	Overs* bowled	Average* no. of overs in day	Average* no. of runs in day	Average no. of runs per over	No. of bowlers in match	% of overs by main bowlers	No. of main spin bowlers	% of overs* bowled by spinners
1905	Leeds	Australia	3	1015	32	377	126	338	2·69	12	96·56	5	54·90
1905	Oval	Australia	3	1178	30	341	114	393	3·45	12	95·31	3	34·89
1909	Oval	Australia	3	1120	28	329	110	373	3·40	14	89·06	7	60·18
1926	Lord's	Australia	3	1052	18	411	137	351	2·55	11	99·52	5	56·94
1929	Birmingham	S. Africa	3	974	25	414	138	325	2·35	13	96·62	3	28·74
1929	Lord's	S. Africa	3	1026	33	364	121	342	2·81	13	94·79	3	29·39
1929	Oval	S. Africa	3	1014	19	354	118	335	2·86	13	92·10	4	45·19
1931	Lord's	N. Zealand	3	1293	34	421	140	431	3·07	11	96·20	5	54·63
1933	Manchester	W. Indies	3	974	30	337	112	325	2·59	14	94·96	4	43·91
1934	Manchester	Australia	4	1307	20	471	118	327	2·77	12	97·67	4	44·79
1935	Leeds	S. Africa	3	875	32	356	119	292	2·45	13	98·04	3	32·86
1935	Manchester	S. Africa	3	1075	28	352	117	358	3·05	14	94·32	3	34·94
1935	Oval	S. Africa	3	1297	22	351	117	432	3·69	13	91·17	3	32·19
1937	Lord's	N. Zealand	3	1120	32	386	129	373	2·90	13	98·19	3	32·64
1938	Nottingham	Australia	4	1496	24	513	128	374	2·91	12	99·74	6	67·05
1938	Lord's	Australia	4	1362	34	380	95	341	3·58	10	97·64	4	47·36
1947	Nottingham	S. Africa	4	1458	31	587	147	385	2·48	13	98·64	5	57·88

1947	Oval	S. Africa	4	1477	33	539	135	369	2·74	13	96·85	5	58·07
1949	Leeds	N. Zealand	3	1175	26	363	121	392	3·23	14	93·94	4	44·62
1949	Lord's	N. Zealand	3	1103	24	366	122	368	2·99	13	93·17	4	54·37
1949	Manchester	N. Zealand	3	1081	26	366	122	360	2·95	16	93·45	4	38·52
1949	Oval	N. Zealand	3	1135	29	327	109	378	3·47	12	99·09	4	37·00
1953	Lord's	Australia	5	1368	37	526	105	274	2·60	13	99·24	3	29·27
1957	Birmingham	W. Indies	5	1315	31	589	118	263	2·23	13	100·00	7	53·65
1957	Nottingham	W. Indies	5	1422	27	538	108	284	2·64	15	94·24	5	37·54
1964	Manchester	Australia	5	1271	18	551	110	254	2·64	14	97·83	4	37·74
1965	Oval	S. Africa	5	1110	34	432	86	222	2·56	11	99·08	3	28·70
1968	Leeds	Australia	5	1159	34	519	104	232	2·23	13	92·49	3	36·41
1969	Lord's	W. Indies	5	1314	36	518	104	263	2·53	13	99·04	2	26·83
1972	Nottingham	Australia	5	1118	28	447	89	224	2·50	13	91·50	3	15·88
1973	Lord's	N. Zealand	5	1267	28	507	101	253	2·49	13	98·62	4	41·81
1973	Birmingham	W. Indies	5	1116	32	477	95	223	2·33	14	93·93	3	33·96
1974	Oval	Pakistan	5	1239	21	421	84	248	2·94	12	99·53	3	31·59
1975	Lord's	Australia	5	1348	30	422	84	270	3·19	13	94·55	2	26·77
1975	Oval	Australia	6	1301	31	501	84	216	2·59	15	91·62	3	31·33
1976	Nottingham	W. Indies	5	1158	27	402	80	232	2·88	15	85·08	1	8·45
1979	Oval	India	5	1270	36	472	94	254	2·69	12	96·62	3	32·62
1981	Oval	Australia	5	1271	36	442	88	254	2·87	9	98·20	2	21·26

*Indicates that figures concerned have either been rounded up to the nearest whole number or, as regards the percentages, figures that gave the percentage were rounded up. NB In some cases no rounding up was necessary.

play have a much better record. The most remarkable of these matches (with high over-rates) were:

Season	Ground	Duration of play	Average no. of overs per day
1905	Leeds	3	126
1926	Lord's	3	137
1929	Birmingham	3	138
1931	Lord's	3	140
1937	Lord's	3	129
1938	Nottingham	4	128
1947	Nottingham	4	147
1947	Oval	4	135

The best in a match (drawn) of five days was the 118-over average at Birmingham in 1957. That was an exception for, as can be seen, many such matches resulted in far less than 100 overs a day. The nearer we come to the present time, the lower the over-rate has become. Indeed 96 overs per day, the agreed rate in England since 1982, has been a considerable improvement!

Hand-in-hand, inevitably, with the reduction in overs bowled was the reduction in runs scored. The dizzy heights of more than 430 runs per day on average at Lord's in 1931 and at The Oval in 1935 seem amazing by today's standards. All the other three-day and four-day Tests produced very commendable figures, yet not one of the five-day games has produced an average of even 300 runs in a single day.

During the Oval Test of 1935 England and South Africa totalled 1297 runs in just three days from the 351 overs. In ten of the five-day Tests listed that run total was not attained, although there were two more days of cricket. Furthermore, they all had vastly more than 351 overs.

A similar pattern is evident from the average number of runs scored from an over. In twelve of the seventeen three-day matches the 'runs per over' reached 2.8 or more, while only four of the fifteen five-day Tests achieved a scoring rate of that degree. So, quite simply, more runs were scored from an over in the shorter matches.

Where do spinners fit into the equation? The five-day matches provide only one example of slow bowlers delivering more than fifty per cent of the overs and that was at Birmingham in 1957, the famous game when May and Cowdrey combated the mysterious skills of Sonny Ramadhin, who set records for bowling the most balls in an international match; Laker and Lock also dominated in the England bowling attack. In the shorter games of three and four days there were eight occasions when the spinners delivered more than half the overs; indeed, at The Oval in 1909 the England and Australian spin bowlers bowled 60.18 per cent and, even more remarkably, the four-day match in 1938 at Nottingham saw the same countries produce 67.05 per cent of the overs from the spinners. Gradually spinners have become less fashionable. West Indies have in recent years seldom played one at all, another reason to hope that all the Test-playing countries will adopt the principle of an acceptable minimum of overs per day.

Unfortunately not all countries are committed to the crucial cause of hastening over-rates. I should like to see England leading the way to a firm reversal of the sluggish trends of the 1970s. In fine weather, a minimum of 110 overs in a six-and-a-half, or seven-hour day should be easily attainable, provided at least 36 overs have been bowled by lunch after a two and a half hour morning session, and at least 72 by tea. After all, limited-overs international matches are now generally 55 (i.e. 110) over games. In this way the duration of Tests could be cut down from five days to four, thus reducing wear and tear on players (though the four days would be very intensive) and making available an extra day, or two days if there is no rest day during the Test, for county and touring matches. By cutting out the uneconomic fifth day, overhead expenses would be reduced and, equally important, the cricket played should be more urgent than it sometimes is at present.

77

SEVEN

Test Cricket
Around the World

The period from 1963 to 1983 began with West Indies laying claim to the title of world champions. Although they lost the final of the 1983 World Cup, few would have argued that they were not still, day in, day out, the best side in the world at the end of it.

Memories of the Brisbane tie, and the pulsating series between Benaud's Australia and Worrell's West Indies, were still fresh when the shortly to be knighted West Indian captain brought his team to England in 1963. They took part in another epic match, the draw at Lord's in which all four results were still possible when the last ball was bowled, then completed a three-one win in the series which clearly proved them to be the stronger side. Peter May's great England side of the mid-1950s had broken up and, although men of the calibre of Dexter, Barrington, Cowdrey (until his arm was broken by a ball from Wes Hall at Lord's), Statham, Trueman, Lock and Titmus remained, the West Indies team lacked only a second top-class opening batsman to go in first with Conrad Hunte. Apart from Hunte, however, there were class batsmen in Worrell himself; Gary (later Sir Garfield) Sobers; Rohan Kanhai; Basil Butcher and Seymour Nurse; plus a dependable young wicket-keeper in Deryck Murray, who stayed on into the next era of West Indian domination; a fearsome fast attack in Hall and Charlie Griffith, supported by the left-arm fast-medium of Sobers and Worrell; and, not least, the most prolific Test spinner in the history of the game, Lance Gibbs, who had support again from Sobers as either an orthodox left-arm slow bowler or as a purveyor of back-of-the-hand spin.

Because of Sobers, the most versatile all-rounder ever, and Gibbs, Worrell's side was a good deal more tactically flexible than the one captained with such success in the 1970s by Clive Lloyd. But Lloyd himself, the long-limbed, bespectacled left-hander, a phenomenally powerful hitter and miraculous cover-fielder in his youth, would have found a place in Worrell's side at four or five and he had a better opening pair – first Greenidge and Fredericks, then Greenidge and Haynes – and four top-class fast bowlers rather than two. In a decade as captain between 1974–75 and 1983–84 Lloyd had an amazingly wide choice from Andy Roberts, Michael Holding, Colin Croft, Sylvester Clarke, Wayne Daniel, Joel Garner, Vanburn Holder, Bernard Julien, Malcolm Marshall, Winston Davis and Eldine Baptiste. Goodish spin bowlers were available and one especially good one, Roger Harper, was developing fast in the early 1980s, but they were seldom used. To balance his fierce, remorseless attack, Lloyd had the greatest batsman in the world in Viv Richards. With Richards to maul one flank of an opposing side and his fast bowlers, Roberts and Holding usually to the fore, to rip apart the other, Lloyd was like a general operating a pincer attack on his hapless enemies.

Richards himself, whom I first saw giving a joyous thrashing to the England bowlers in Antigua in 1974, the year he first appeared for Somerset, developed dramatically in 1976 at the age of twenty-four. In that calendar year he scored 1710 runs in nineteen Test innings at an average of 90, with seven centuries. Not since Bradman had it seemed so inevitable that a batsman would dominate any big occasion.

The West Indies did suffer a bad patch in the middle of the period, losing to Australia in 1968–69, 1973, and, in a battle of giants, again in 1975–76. They lost also to England in 1968 and 1969 and even at home to India in 1971.

Victories by India away from their own soil had in the past been infrequent but under the phlegmatic captaincy of a solid left-handed batsman from Bombay, Ajit Wadekar, and with four superb spin bowlers – the off-spinners, Erapally Prasanna and Srinivasaraghavan Venkataraghavan (a satisfying mouth-

ful for a commentator), the classical slow left-armer, Bishen
Bedi, and the unorthodox medium-paced leg-spinner, Bhag-
wat Chandrasekhar – India were a match for anyone. They
were supported by the most prolific of all the prolific opening
batsmen of the era, Sunil Gavaskar, who began his Test career
in the West Indies in 1970–71 with scores of 65, 67 not out,
116, 64 not out, 1, 117 not out, 124 and 220 not out. In both
1976 and 1978 he passed 1000 Test runs in a calendar year
and this brave, orthodox, compact, masterly little batsman
passed, in 1983–84, both Geoff Boycott and Gary Sobers as
the highest scorer in all Test cricket. He also equalled Don
Bradman's twenty-nine Test hundreds, but it took him eighty-
seven more innings to do so!

Wadekar's side also won a rubber in England for the first
time, in 1971, but not until 1983 did India enjoy a moment of
equally giddy success, their triumph in the third Prudential
World Cup when, against all odds and most logical expecta-
tions, they overcame West Indies in the final. Gavaskar was
still there, his period as captain over, but his great batting
contemporary, the tiny, piratical Gundappa Viswanath of the
flashing cuts and square-drives, was now out of form and
favour after a record number of eighty-seven consecutive
appearances in Tests. At the centre now was the charismatic
figure of Kapil Dev, the tall, military-looking fast bowler and
powerful, clean-hitting batsman, round whom a capable team
had been built up. Team was the word. India had not always
played with harmony of purpose but they did so now despite
the fact that apart from Kapil Dev, Gavaskar, the wicket-
keeper Kirmani, and Mohinder Amarnath, a calm, well-
organised batsman, none of the team would have been considered indisputably a world-class player.

Team spirit has always in the past been one of the great
strengths of Australian sides but the traditional togetherness of
this nation of individualists once they pulled on a baggy green
cap was disrupted by the Packer affair. For this reason Australian performances between 1977 and 1983 were curiously
unpredictable, despite the fact that Dennis Lillee and Greg

The Packer Revolution was caused by the ruthless determination of the Australian businessman Kerry Packer (left) to bulldoze his way into securing the rights of his television company, Channel Nine, to cover Australian Test cricket. Here he makes his way to the High Court in London prior to his successful bid to prevent the cricketing authorities from 'banning' his contracted players from 'official' cricket.

Tony Greig (right), sacked as England captain for his role as a recruiting agent for Packer, became captain of the Rest of the World team in World Series Cricket. Here he has a net under the critical eye of Sir Garfield Sobers.
Press Association; Adrian Murrell/All-Sport

Greig (left) became a television commentator for Channel Nine on his retirement from cricket. Here he reports on the state of the pitch, one of many innovations in the Australian style of cricket coverage on television, designed to attract a wide audience, and not afraid of gimmicks.

Intimidatory fast bowling was commonplace in WSC cricket and spread through international cricket thereafter. Mike Brearley (right) was one of the first to use the helmet, now almost *de rigeur* for all batsman in Test matches.
Adrian Murrell/All-Sport

South Africa's isolation from world cricket stirred deep emotions. Basil D'Oliveira (left), a superb all-round cricketer, was refused entry by the Nationalist Government for England's proposed tour of 1968-69.

The planned tour by South Africa to England in 1970 was eventually called off by the Labour Government for fear of disruption by anti-apartheid demonstrators. This protest (right) took place outside The Oval during the Surrey v Northamptonshire match on 2 May, 1970.
Patrick Eagar; Press Association

In 1981 Robin Jackman (left) of Surrey, an Englishman who played much winter cricket in South Africa, was served a deportation order by the Guyana Government. The Test match at Georgetown did not, therefore, take place.

In 1982-83 a West Indian team played international cricket against South Africa for the first time in history. The West Indian captain, Lawrence Rowe (right), was banned for life from official West Indian cricket, along with the rest of his team. *Adrian Murrell/All-Sport*

One-day cricket brought back the crowds to county cricket...Lord's packed for the Lancashire v Sussex Gillette Cup final of 1970. These two counties were the first to be revived by their success at the limited-overs game.
Sport & General

If it did nothing for batting techniques and damage to attacking bowling, limited-overs cricket nevertheless did wonders for outfielding. Here Graham Barlow, one of the finest cover-points of his generation, attempts to run out David Thomas in the 1980 final between Middlesex and Surrey, the last final under the patronage of Gillette. *Adrian Murrell/All-Sport*

The start of it all. Ted Dexter, an 'amateur' captain in the first year of fully professional English cricket, holds the Gillette Cup aloft after the 1963 final. *Sport & General*

Big brother is watching you. Attendances in the first year of WSC cricket were
sparse by Australian standards, despite intense publicity. The spectators at
UFL Park in Melbourne were swamped by outsized portraits of Clive Lloyd,
Ian Chappell and Tony Greig, captains of the competing teams.
Adrian Murrell/All-Sport

Australian 'official cricket' jumped on the WSC bandwaggon, apparently
believing that the game was not enough of an attraction in itself without
professional marketing. A pop group 'entertains' the crowd at Sydney (left)
during a one-day international in December 1979.

   Night cricket (right) did not catch on in the colder climate of England. Here
Clive Lloyd plays beneath the lights of Chelsea Football Club at Stamford
Bridge. Lancashire won the one and only 'Lambert and Butler Floodlight Cup'.
Adrian Murrell/All-Sport

Umpires have earned their money during the last twenty years. Syd Buller (left), who caused a stir by no-balling the South African fast bowler Geoff Griffin during an exhibition match at Lord's in 1960, walking out with Arthur Fagg, who temporarily refused to continue standing in a Test at Edgbaston in 1973 because of the open dissent of several of the West Indies team after he had refused an appeal against Geoff Boycott.

No one in the last twenty years (or indeed in history) has taken so many Test wickets as Dennis Lillee (right). Nor has anyone appealed with such aggression. *Sport & General; Adrian Murrell/All-Sport*

The Saturday of the second of the Centenary Tests, at Lord's in 1980, saw English cricket's public relations at its worst. A full house, a sunny day, a wet ground, stubborn umpires, insensitive players, a furious crowd, and harrassed administrators. The dramatis personae in this midfield conference are Jim Fairbrother (groundsman) Ian Botham (England captain) Col John Stephenson (MCC Assistant Secretary) umpires Bird and Constant and Greg Chappell (Australian captain). *Adrian Murrell/All-Sport*

Belligerence and dissent. Two of the less welcome features of modern cricket displayed by Graham Dilley (England) and Rodney Marsh (Australia) during a one-day international in 1979.   *Adrian Murrell/All-Sport*

Dennis Lillee (left) was a wonderful fast-bowler who could at times be a blustering prima donna. In the Perth Test against England in 1979-80 he argued heatedly when the umpires ordered him to exchange a conventional bat for the aluminium one which he was using in the match for publicity purposes. The game was held up for ten minutes but the Australian Cricket Board subsequently failed to take serious action.

   Aggression is not exclusively Australian! A supercharged Ian Botham (right), England's finest all-rounder since Wally Hammond, bowls Rodney Hogg in the First Test at Brisbane, 1978-79.   *Adrian Murrell/All-Sport*

The age of commercialism. The England team in Australia in 1982-83 were
sponsored by a Japanese-based audio/video firm. Left to right: D.W. Randall,
G. Fowler, C. J. Tavaré, R. D. Jackman, G. Miller, V. J. Marks (seated) N. G.
Cowans, D. I. Gower, R. G. D. Willis, I. T. Botham, D. R. Pringle, N. G. B.
Cook, I .J. Gould (seated), E. E. Hemmings, A. J. Lamb, R. W. Taylor.

Dreaming of an equally wealthy future? Or just the honour of playing for their
country? The England Young Cricketers of 1983, hoping to be household
names before long. Standing: S.J. Rhodes, P. W. Jarvis, R. A. Pick, G. D. Rose,
G. V. Palmer, P. Such, P. A. Smith. Seated: G.R. Cowdrey, N. H. Fairbrother,
H. Morris, P. J. Pritchard, J. E. Morris.

Chappell, who retired together at the end of the 1983–84 season, were two men who would have been written into any contemporary World XI. Both had been key figures in one of the toughest and most successful of Australian sides, that led by Greg's brother, Ian. As with most powerful Test sides their success was founded on fast bowlers – the combination of Lillee and Jeff Thomson, though short-lived, being one of the most formidable in history. These two overwhelmed England in 1974–75 and the following year proved too good also for Lloyd's West Indians, whose own pace attack had not yet reached maturity.

Ian Chappell himself was, though a less classical and graceful batsman than his taller younger brother, a tenacious and talented player and, again like his brother, a brilliant slip fielder. To support his fast bowlers – of whom Lillee, with his long, menacing run, superb, leaping action, immense strength and perfect control of pace, swing and cut, was arguably the best of all time – Chappell had a big-hearted Tasmanian-born swing bowler, Max Walker, and at times a talented, left-handed all-rounder in the Alan Davidson mould, Gary Gilmour. Ashley Mallett was an accurate off-spin bowler, one of the few really good ones Australia has produced, and, for a while at least, John Gleeson, Terry Jenner, Kerry O'Keeffe, and Jim Higgs kept alive the great Australian tradition of leg-spin bowling.

Lillee and Thomson, at least the equal of the other two most famous Australian fast-bowling combinations, Gregory and MacDonald and Lindwall and Miller, were supported by several brilliant close catchers – notably the Chappell brothers, Ian Redpath, Mallett, and Doug Walters – while in the covers Paul Sheahan and Ross Edwards were both superb.

If the side which in successive seasons in the mid-1970s overwhelmed Mike Denness's England and Clive Lloyd's West Indies had a weakness, it was at the start of the innings, although Redpath played many a staunch innings. He was not, however, the equal of either Bob Simpson or Bill Lawry, the prolific opening pair who had made up for relatively modest bowling in the Australian teams of the 1960s. The exception was Graham McKenzie, a fast bowler of great strength with a classical action who took 246 wickets at an average of 29 each despite being the only shock bowler in the side in a Test career lasting from 1961 to 1971. His best support came from Neil Hawke and Alan Connolly. Two outstanding wicket-keepers, Wally Grout and Rodney Marsh, did duty behind the stumps through the best part of two decades – the rugged Marsh staying on to break all records both for victims and longevity. He retired after the 1983–84 season with 355 Test dismissals. And there were many fine middle-order batsmen, other than those already mentioned. At the start of the period there were Brian Booth, Peter Burge and Bob Cowper, one of Test cricket's ten triple-hundred makers; a little later came Sheahan and Walters, an exemplary sportsman and a brilliantly incisive stroke-player who twice scored at least 100 runs in a Test session, a rare achievement; and latterly three left-handers, Allan Border, David Hookes and Graham Yallop, plus a gifted right-hander, Kim Hughes.

Australia may have had more success than not in the years after 1963 but they also experienced some of their greatest humiliations, notably in 1966–67 and 1970 at the hands of South Africa, who had just developed the finest side in their history when politics took them out of Test cricket. This is saying much, because South Africa's teams in the early 1960s had always been talented and attractive, with high-class players in Jackie McGlew, Roy McLean, Trevor Goddard, John Waite, Colin Bland (unforgettable as a cover fielder), Hugh Tayfield, Neil Adcock and Peter Heine. But the side which in the early months of 1970 murdered their Australian visitors by four Tests to nil, each game won by a huge margin, ranks with some of the best elevens from any nation at any time.

Barry Richards and Graeme Pollock are two of the finest batsmen of the century, while Denis Lindsay was a prolific wicket-keeper batsman, Mike Procter an all-rounder of the highest class (similar to but superior, in my opinion, at his height to Imran Khan), and Eddie Barlow was also a fine all-rounder who made absolutely everything of his abilities. Only Tony Greig in recent times has been Barlow's equal for making things happen on a cricket field the way he wanted them to: Barlow's belligerent swing bowling complemented well the fierce pace of Procter and Peter Pollock. The side was particularly well captained by Dr Ali Bacher and although there was no spinner in the Tayfield class, John Traicos from Rhodesia showed much promise in the brief Test career he was allowed before bobbing up again as a member of the Zimbabwe team in the 1983 World Cup.

England have always been a difficult team to beat in home conditions but their performances abroad in the last two decades have been modest on the whole despite some notable exceptions. One was a narrow victory in the rubber in South Africa in 1964–65, when the doughty Ken Barrington, one of the most dependable batsmen England ever had, enjoyed a good series, as did the gifted, left-handed opening batsman, Bob Barber, who, like Barrington, was also a useful leg-break bowler. This England side also included Ted Dexter, a marvellously commanding batsman of the highest class; and Geoff Boycott, just starting to establish himself as first choice to open the England innings and on the way to proving himself the most single-minded accumulator of runs in his, perhaps in any, era.

A strong batting side was completed by M. J. K. Smith, a tall, inventive player and excellent captain; Jim Parks, a talented batsman who made himself into a wicket-keeper who seldom let England down; and Peter Parfitt, a brilliant fielder close to the wicket and, in the mood, a handsome left-handed batsman. There were two good off-spinners, Titmus and David Allen, but apart from 'big Dave' – D. J. Brown of Warwickshire – the fast bowling attack was thin.

Another notable overseas triumph, equally unexpected, was that in the West Indies in 1967–68 under Colin Cowdrey, that devoted cricketer and richly gifted batsman with the timing of a great musician. The fast bowling was now greatly strengthened by the wiry, rhythmic John Snow and the hostile, left-armed Welshman Jeff Jones – and the batting was all the more classy for the presence of Tom Graveney, gracious and elegant from the boundary, but devilish hard to get out once he had got a start in the middle.

Three years later Cowdrey had lost the captaincy through injury and Ray Illingworth, who had quickly seized the chance to prove himself a tough, astute leader, took the side to Australia instead. With Boycott now at his peak and Snow too, England were too strong for their opponents; but though England held the Ashes in a memorable drawn series in 1972, they were to be regained with a vengeance by Australia under Ian Chappell two years later.

The pendulum swung England's way again rather faster than might have been the case had not Mr Packer's promotions upset the Australian applecart. Under the razor-sharp captaincy of Mike Brearley, England, with bright new talent emerging after a fallow period in David Gower, Graham Gooch and, above all, Ian Botham, overcame Greg Chappell's unsettled 1977 touring team and then crushed the Australian second eleven in 1978–79 by five games to one. Three excellent fast-medium bowlers – Chris Old, John Lever and Mike Hendrick – and two gifted spinners from Middlesex, John Emburey and Phil Edmonds, shared in the rout. Not that the Australian second eleven was without talent: in Hughes, Yallop, Hogg, who had an amazingly successful first series as a fast bowler, taking 41 wickets, Border, and the off-spinner, Bruce Yardley, Australia were blooding some useful players for the future.

Brearley had succeeded as captain the South African born Tony Greig, six foot seven inches of cricketing grit. Most of Greig's finest hours were spent overseas in England's cause, notably when inspiring England to a drawn series under the captaincy of Mike Denness against West Indies in 1974, and when captaining them to an unexpected victory in India in 1976–77. Two of his most reliable colleagues on these tours were Dennis Amiss, a staunch and attractive batsman, and Alan Knott, a superbly agile little wicket-keeper and a daring, determined, unorthodox batsman with a streak of impish genius.

Many of the most talented players of the period came from Pakistan, though their performances were frequently undermined by the Machiavellian intrigues amongst players and administrators. Their former captain, Abdul Hafeez Kardar, was for many years the chief power in Pakistan cricket and one who would have liked a stronger influence also in the conduct of world cricket. He walked out of an International Cricket Conference meeting in 1974 because Israel had been appointed an associate member.

Such was the bickering and back-stabbing in Pakistan dressing-rooms that one could seldom be sure of any tour to or from that country passing without incident or controversy. No country changes its Test captain so often and in 1983–84 Imran Khan, chosen amidst the inevitable controversy to lead the side to Australia, had three other recent Test captains under his command: Zaheer Abbas, Javed Miandad (unseated by a players' revolt) and Wasim Bari, a long-serving and excellent wicket-keeper who had taken charge when most of the top players signed for Mr Packer.

But if Pakistan seldom jelled as a team it equally seldom mattered, especially at home, for they turned out world-class players almost as often as West Indies. Imran Khan's prowess has already been mentioned. He had a useful partner, and predecessor, in the tall Pathan, Sarfraz Nawaz, an engaging eccentric who was always in trouble with someone in authority. Towards the end of the period Pakistan also produced perhaps the best international leg-spinner since Richie Benaud in Abdul Qadir, though Intikhab Alam, a calm, steady figure amongst all the intrigues and a fine captain on the 1974 tour to England, was also a consistent back-of-the-hand spinner (and a strong batsman) who earned the respect of the best players.

It was the batsmen, however, who really bore the proud torch of Pakistan cricket through the 1960s and 1970s: Zaheer Abbas, Majid Khan, Asif Iqbal, Hanif Mohammad and his brother Mushtaq, and Javed Miandad were all players from the very top drawer. Wasim Raja, Sadiq Mohammad and the opening pair of recent vintage, Mudassar Nazar and Mohsin Khan, were only a little behind them.

Finally into the Test fold, after years knocking patiently on the door, came Sri Lanka, the beautiful island off the south coast of India which, since staging an inaugural Test against England in 1982, has had its problems, but also its moments. A good leg-spinner in Somachandra De Silva, and fine batsmen in Duleep Mendis and Roy Dias in particular have maintained a long tradition of cricket in Ceylon, though it is doubtful whether the game on the island is played any better now than it used to be when the country took on the occasional touring team on its way to or from England or Australia. If only because they bring variety, however, Sri Lanka are a welcome addition to the brotherhood of Test cricketers. Brotherhood it is, and would cheerfully remain so if only cricket could be played in isolation from a world steadily more affected and obsessed by international politics. This is a subject which can be avoided no longer.

EIGHT

The Problem
of South Africa

In his admirable book *In Defence of Politics*, Professor Bernard Crick argues:

'The attempt to politicise everything is the destruction of politics. When everything is seen as relevant to politics, then politics has in fact become totalitarianism . . . to ensure that there be politics at all, there must be some things which are irrelevant to politics.'

In its simplest terms, the perennial debate about whether or not cricketers should play with or against South Africans boils down to whether sport should be one of man's activities that is free of politics. Whatever moral stand one takes in answering that question, however, events in the last fifteen years have proved that politicians are more powerful than sportsmen. In some countries, at least, it is *impossible* for sport to exist in isolation from government policies. Yet, paradoxically, the whole emphasis of the opponents of South Africa's apartheid policies has been on recognising the power of sport to change those policies: in other words, sport is a powerful political weapon.

The question, once that is accepted, is altered. Is it right to use sport as a weapon, to the detriment of sportsmen of all colours, if those who use the weapon are not prepared to make sacrifices in other fields which affect themselves? It is all very well for a trader in arms, or stainless steel, or toys, or all the other articles sent to South Africa, to support the sporting isolation of that country on moral grounds. But what would be their attitude if their own livelihood was at stake? All but a high-principled few, of course, would find a ban on their own sales to South Africa insupportable. This is true even of South Africa's most implacable opponents. For example, the Russians have close secret links with South Africa's most powerful gold and diamond merchants: the bulk of the world's gold, diamonds and platinum happens to lie under the earth of these two countries and it pays both to collude to keep world prices as high as possible. Yet politically each country deplores the other's regime.

Whether it is more uncomfortable to be a Bantu in Johannesburg or a Jew in Moscow is a moot point. But because political opposition to South Africa, a democracy for whites only (though in the new 1984 constitution 'coloureds' and Indians were given a limited share), is better organised than it is to the Soviet Union, a democracy for no one, it is considered wrong to play cricket against South Africa yet right to play soccer against Russia. To underline this inconsistency, I saw a Johannesburg Jew, called Mandy Yachad, making his first appearance for South Africa against the unofficial West Indian team in 1984. He would not have played for his country had he instead been a Russian footballer.

Equally inconsistent is the fact that cricket has to bear the brunt of the sporting boycott of South Africa. Professional golfers, for example, go and play there for huge prize-money without being penalised other than to be placed on a 'black list' drawn up by the United Nations Committee against Apartheid. Motor racing drivers do likewise. And the captain of the British Lions Rugby Union team to South Africa in 1980, Bill Beaumont, was given an OBE soon after his return, despite the fact that the British government disapproved officially of the tour. Yet fifteen English cricketers who toured the Republic for a month in 1982 on a tour sponsored by South African Breweries were banned for three years by the TCCB, largely because it was considered economically necessary to ensure that the Cricket Boards of West Indies, India and Pakistan did not, under the orders of their own governments, refuse to play against an England side including these men.

The threat of a split between the 'white' and 'black' cricketing countries has become serious in recent years. In the West Indies in 1981, England were obliged to leave Guyana in a hurry because one member of the touring team, Robin Jackman, had South African connections. (Born in India of British parents, he had played for several winters for Rhodesia and married a South African girl. He later settled in South Africa.) The West Indies Cricket Board withdrew an invitation to New Zealand to tour because New Zealand's rugby team had been to South Africa. And in 1983 they also scuppered a planned tour to the Caribbean by England's women cricketers, because a few members of the selected touring party had some time previously been on a private visit to South Africa. Not long afterwards the West Indies Cricket Board forbade their team, who were in England for the 1983 World Cup, to play against a Yorkshire side containing two of the fifteen men who had been on the South African Breweries tour. Yet the same West Indies Board had voted the previous year, through their representatives at the ICC meeting, not to dictate to any other country whom they might or might not select for their teams. As Michael Melford forcibly put it in *The Cricketer*:

'If some countries do not wish to play against South Africa, that is their business but they have no right to object to English or New Zealand teams doing so.'

Hypocrisies and inconsistencies abound in this matter. Up to 1980 Rhodesia, like South Africa, was banned from participation in most world sport. Yet a change of government, from one dominated by whites to another dominated by one black tribe, has automatically made the land now called Zimbabwe acceptable. Argentina, with whom, officially, Britain was still at war in June 1983, attended the ICC meeting at Lord's, whereas South Africa, who fought with Britain in the last world war, was forbidden even to put its case for re-entry. Yet it was not the South African Cricket Union which was playing at politics. Their representatives, led by the determined, reasonable and courteous Joe Pamensky, merely asked that, having been expelled from international cricket after

1970 until they achieved multi-racial cricket at all levels, they should now be allowed back in on the grounds that they had achieved that goal.

There is no doubt whatsoever that South African sportsmen have been forced into making changes because of the effectiveness of the sporting boycott against them. When the South African Catholic Bishops' Conference declared its opposition to the Springboks' tour of New Zealand in May 1981, it stated that: 'We wish to encourage all attempts to bring about real change in South Africa by non-violent means. Sports boycotts are an effective means of applying pressure for change.'

Few would argue that more change is not desirable, despite the progress towards 'genuinely multi-racial' sport. Classification of a person's colour at birth is abhorrent and the dice are still heavily loaded against the vast majority of those unfortunate enough to be born 'coloured', 'Indian' or 'African', the offensive official government classifications.

Those of us who abhor the idea of apartheid, yet believe in the rights of individual sportsmen and women to play with and against whom they please, have to decide whether this individual freedom should be sacrificed in the fight for the civil and human rights of citizens in South Africa. But this gives rise to another crucial question: is the sporting boycott still helping to force the South African government into relaxing those apartheid laws, which split families and force the black population into membership of artificial 'homelands' often miles away from the place in which they were born and raised; or has the boycott now become counter-productive, by encouraging a reaction against liberalisation of the apartheid laws from right-wing extremists like the *Afrikaaner Weerstandsbeweging* party?

Even if one accepts that the changes in South African sport in general, and cricket in particular, since isolation began in 1970 have merely been 'cosmetic', they have surely increased rather than decreased the possibility of changes in other spheres of South African life.

Certain determined opponents of apartheid, such as the

strong political group SACOS (South African Committee of Sport) and one of its leading figures, Hassan Howa, with his famous 'no normal sport in an abnormal society' motto, have refused to co-operate in new sporting bodies purporting to speak for sportsmen of all hues. No doubt they are right, in one way, to be suspicious of government liberalisations in sport. After all, the laws themselves, such as the Group Areas and Liquor acts, have not changed for the majority. Clubs and sports associations have to seek government permission by licence to organise racially mixed fixtures and facilities. But if there is some reason to doubt the government's sincerity, there is little to doubt that of the sporting administrators who have worked so hard, especially in cricket, to give coloured and African players a better opportunity to enjoy and become good at the game. Only one example is the former chairman of Western Province Cricket Club, John Passmore, who for many years has devoted himself to encouraging the development of African cricketers, enlisting the support of white coaches including many visiting English county cricketers. I saw at first hand early in 1984 the pretty little ground he has helped to create, with enthusiastic local support, in the African township of Langa, just outside Cape Town. It is an oasis amongst the surrounding squalor and several good African players have developed there.

Recently, of course, African interest in cricket has also been encouraged by the policy of the South African Cricket Union in offering large sums of money to West Indian cricketers to tour South Africa, using the Packer principle that every man has his price. In fact a good many of the leading West Indian stars turned down huge sums (dismissed by some as 'blood money') but others found themselves unable to refuse what they considered a legitimate business proposition. Professional cricketers, they argued, had a right to play for whoever would pay them most to play, just like any other professional. And so successful was the first tour, in 1982–83, that they could go home believing with good reason that they had done something for the dignity of the black man in South Africa. They were missionaries as well as mercenaries, though from what I saw the following year they did not take their evangelical duties too seriously! The fact remains, however, that they attracted wide interest from people of all colours, and the sight of young white South Africans playing games of cricket naturally with African boys on the outfield during a four-day 'Test' at Port Elizabeth was tangible evidence to weigh against the claims that these games provided an illusion of normality whilst the important laws of apartheid remained.

In 1983, MCC members were asked to vote, at a special general meeting in London, on a proposition to send a private MCC team to South Africa. This forced many of us who had been inclined to sit on the fence on a difficult issue to come down, and to try to reach a conclusion.

On one hand, members had the advice of their committee, many of whom felt a firm duty to 'keep Test cricket as played by the ICC countries alive'. An MCC tour, if exploited by political interests hostile to the thought of 'normal cricket in an abnormal society', would, it was argued by the majority of committee members, place in jeopardy not only the future of Test cricket, but also, through loss of vital finance, many of the seventeen first-class counties. Moreover, it would threaten the position of MCC as a private club with a public responsibility. There was a theoretical threat, too, to Test cricket at Lord's, the most famous cricket ground in the world, and a corresponding threat to the traditional role of MCC as chairman of the International Cricket Conference and as guardian of the Laws of the Game.

On the other hand, members had to consider both their consciences and the paper sent to them before the vote by the group, led by John Carlisle, who were seeking to send the private MCC team. This group felt a moral obligation to do something positive to encourage the South African cricket community after their successful efforts to introduce multi-racial cricket. They reiterated that it was hypocritical to trade with South Africa, yet not play cricket with her, and wrong for England to be forced into leaving out some of her best players from the Test side purely because they offended certain overseas governments.

I was not, at first, convinced that a tour by MCC was the most helpful plan in the circumstances. What good it would do was questionable and the danger that it might be exploited by politicians and used to disrupt international cricket was real, as was the threat to MCC's position as the leader of the game with an objective and global view of its best interests. On the other hand the tour represented a small but important gesture on the part of sportsmen to preserve their right, in a free country, to play against whom they pleased.

However, the political aspect had to be considered. What, I have asked myself all along since 1968, is so special about the evil of apartheid, compared with, for example, the repression of anyone in Eastern Europe with 'unofficial' opinions? How, except in its petty application – the absurd idea, now, as far as I could see in 1984, almost dead, that a black should go through one door, a white through another – how does apartheid differ fundamentally from the persecution of one tribe by another in other parts of Africa or, even in the apparently civilised world of cricket, the continuing enforced subservience of the untouchables in India or of Asians in Guyana? All these people are, from birth, like some of Orwell's animals, 'less equal than others'.

Just because evils exist in other countries, people cannot be prevented from endeavouring to persuade the South African government that enforced segregation of the races is morally wrong – however much one appreciates the dangers of changing the old order too quickly. But the idea of cutting South Africa out of world sport has served its purpose at least in a sporting context. In 1968 Basil D'Oliveira was refused entry to play cricket for England in South Africa; now he or any other coloured cricketer is welcome. That is the extent of the change that has taken place. Whether or not the change has been the result of South Africa's sporting isolation, the time has surely come to build on the progress already made by encouraging cricket contacts. If you give a man no hope of a job when he comes out of gaol, the chances are that he will return to crime. This, at any rate, was the conclusion I came to after much heart-searching and an attempt to weigh my belief in a free society with my passion for cricket. One of the roles of MCC has always been the propagation of the game everywhere in the world, and to my mind the tour needed to be viewed in that context. When, later, I saw for myself the determination of white South African cricket officials to foster the game amongst all races through coaching and the staging of international matches, I was further convinced that sporting contact does much more good than harm.

In the event, the tour proposal was rejected by a heavy majority of MCC members. It was another blow to South African pride. On the face of it, there seems little prospect of South Africa's rejoining the ICC, and thus playing Test cricket again, until – either by political persuasion or by violent revolution – there is a black government in Pretoria.

This melancholy conclusion grew steadily more obvious through the 1970s. Paradoxically, indeed, the more genuine the claims within South Africa that their cricket was racially mixed at all levels, the more certain it became that the hard-line attitude of the country's political opponents would prevail. The uncompromising attitude of the South African government in the late 1960s when, perhaps, there was still time to nip the sports boycott in the bud by showing a genuine willingness to work for multi-racial sport in the Republic, backfired on them. It was South Africa's critics who were being uncompromising now. The 1970s marked increasingly vigorous attempts by white cricketers and administrators to undo the neglect of years in their apathetic attitude to non-white cricketers. But by the end of that decade the South African Cricket Union, formed in 1977 with the intention of representing cricketers of all colours, had implicitly given up hope of attracting official teams from abroad. Sending their own touring team anywhere they already knew would be impossible, because of demonstrations and disruption by protesters. Instead, the isolation was ended by artificial means. With the help of sponsors in South Africa – and, it was alleged, but never proved and hotly denied, the help also of government money – an English team toured in 1981–82, a Sri Lankan one in 1982–83 (a disastrous exercise for everyone), while a West Indian one visited in 1982–83 and the following year. The West Indians, though not the equal of the current official West Indies Test team, nevertheless contained enough established Test cricketers to attract genuine interest and provide real competition for the leading South African players. Indeed in 1983–84, they proved the stronger team.

Tired of fruitless persuasion, the Springbok, armed with Krugerrands, is now fighting back. It is worth outlining briefly the cricketing and political moves which led to this present deadlock.

British soldiers and settlers brought cricket to South Africa in the nineteenth century and in areas where British influence was strongest, especially in the Cape Province, Africans and Malays also took the game up. But there is evidence of discrimination against cricketers on the grounds of colour as early as 1894 when the Malayan fast bowler, J. 'Krom' Hendricks, was selected to tour England after performing impressively against W. W. Read's touring side, only to be omitted as a result of 'the greatest pressure by those in high authority in the Cape Colony'. No doubt exactly the same attitude would have obtained at the same time in the British West Indies.

In 1904 the South African Coloured Cricket Board was instituted, and matches were played in provincial centres for the Barnato Trophy. Gradually the various racial groups split off to form independent cricketing bodies but in 1947, at the instigation of the Indians, a new grouping of 'black' cricketers was formed, calling itself the South African Cricket Board of Control. Rashid Varachia, later to become President of the SA Cricket Union, was SACBOC's first secretary. In 1958, when Basil D'Oliveira led a pioneering, non-white touring party to East Africa, a meeting of SACBOC decided to integrate the various racial groups – Africans, Coloureds, Indians and

Malays. But when, belatedly, the South African Cricket Association, the white cricket authority, approached the government to propose mixed play between races in 1960, the door was firmly shut in their faces. In 1967, the prime minister, B. J. Vorster, stated bluntly in the House of Assembly that there could be no mixed race sporting events: 'On this matter we are not prepared to compromise, we are not prepared to negotiate and we are not prepared to make concessions.'

It was not long before the National Party government, which enshrined in law the hated policy of apartheid or 'separate development', after its election in 1948, was being forced by the sporting boycott to make the concessions Vorster had refused. But there was much trauma before the liberals started to have their way. The 1968–69 MCC tour was called off by the Cricket Council when Mr Vorster refused to allow Basil D'Oliveira – who had been selected only as a late replacement for Tom Cartwright, though most felt he should have been a certain selection in the first place – to enter the country of his birth. Before long, coloured cricketers were being welcomed to the Republic, but only as 'honorary whites'.

As South African individuals such as Mike Procter and Barry Richards began to invade county cricket after the relaxation of restrictions on overseas players in 1968, the political opposition was gaining in strength. After bitter arguments and an impassioned debate in the House of Commons, not to mention at an MCC special general meeting, the proposed South African tour of the United Kingdom was called off at the behest of the British government. It was already clear before the decision was taken that demonstrators would have disrupted the cricket to an unacceptable degree.

It was really from this point on, whether anyone appreciated the fact or not, that sportsmen lost control of the situation. The South African Cricket Association was told by the Cricket Council that England would not play against them again until cricket was played and teams were selected on a multi-racial basis.

The South African tour to Australia in 1971–72 was also called off and while, by their performances in county cricket, Richards, Procter, Barlow, McEwan, Rice, Kirsten and Van der Bijl later amply proved that even in isolation the country could produce players of world calibre, sports administrators in the Republic worked feverishly to repair the decades of disinterest towards coloured cricketers.

The British businessman, Derrick Robins, kept alive the hopes of continued international relationships by taking touring teams to South Africa which, although predominantly English, also contained some coloured players, notably John Shepherd and Younis Ahmed. As isolation started to bite, the South African government relaxed its uncompromising attitude, allowing the Robins team to play a multi-racial team in 1974–75 and the following season giving permission for an African team to take part in the Gillette Cup. These barriers had only slowly been broken down. As early as 1971 the leading cricketers had demonstrated their opposition to apartheid by walking off the field in the middle of a trial match for the selection of the touring team to Australia.

In 1975–76 nine officials – three from each of the main cricket bodies, European, Indian and African – formed a committee to hasten the day of multi-racial cricket. That season a strong touring side, managed by Richie Benaud and including the Chappell brothers and Mike Denness, played all their games against 'mixed' opposition. But tours to England and Australia planned for the mid-1970s were both cancelled and Boon Wallace, a patient worker for multi-racial cricket, was even refused a visa by an Australian government which had in the past sanctioned cricket regularly against all-white South African cricket without even thinking about it.

Wallace was instrumental, however, in the real administrative breakthrough in January 1976 when the three representative boards came together under the chairmanship of Rashid Varachia. Finally, in September 1977, the South African Cricket Union was formed, with Varachia as President, a post he held until his death in 1981.

In human affairs, however, the personalities of men have an importance often underestimated. A rivalry between Varachia and the flamboyant former leader of SACBOC, Hassan Howa, came to the surface again and Howa led a breakaway group who formed a rival body, the South African Cricket Board. The divisions between these two men, and later the two Boards, have been easily exploited by those who oppose any compromise with South Africa until apartheid has been wiped out altogether, not just from cricket and other sports.

There seems little doubt that although much cricket is played under the auspices of the SACB (generally in poor conditions because of a lack of resources and Mr Howa's policy of turning down financial aid if he suspects it is offered for political reasons), mixed cricket for those who want it *does* exist in South Africa today. In some areas it is easier than in others where talented black players wanting to get ahead are unwilling to risk criticisms that they are 'selling out' to the whites.

Graham Johnson, the long-serving Kent all-rounder, who since 1978 has been helping to coordinate a deep-rooted coaching programme in Johannesburg financed by Barclays Bank, believes that when the people currently at the helm of SACU and SACB retire, the differences between them may be looked upon as a passing phase. 'To say that either camp truly has the support of the non-white cricketer,' Johnson wrote in his article in the 1983 *Wisden*, 'is to over-simplify a complicated issue.'

Johnson's balanced views should be read by anyone wishing to understand the current position of South African cricket. He points to the fact that non-white boys have achieved selection on merit in several age-groups since 1978. But he adds: 'Having established the framework in which equal development and opportunity can take place, there is bound to be a lead-in period before the talent develops sufficiently for the non-white players whom the public expect to see representing South Africa, and playing at provincial level, to do so in any numbers. Initially the non-white representation has to come from the Coloured and Asian groups. Nevertheless, given time, I can see no reason why the development of African cricket should not be along the lines of South African football, which has become an African-dominated sport.'

It is clear from the enthusiastic reception of at least some of the African community of South Africa that the visit of the West Indian 'rebels' in 1982–83 and the following season hastened the day when the efforts of men like John Passmore in Cape Town will be rewarded by the visible success of Africans winning Springbok caps. This in turn would generate 'second phase' enthusiasm amongst young Africans.

It is interesting that many of those who know South Africa intimately are coming to the conclusion that to continue to shut the country off from the rest of world cricket could be counter-productive, both in cricketing and social terms. The game in South Africa, as in other countries, is in danger, because of the isolation, of being taken over by entrepreneurs who see cricket only as a business. The lure of their money could further denude Test teams and hasten the threatened split between those countries who are prepared to have some contact with South Africa and those who are not.

The Gleneagles Agreement, signed at the meeting of Commonwealth foreign ministers in June 1977, committed all the countries concerned to 'take every practical step to discourage' such contacts. To non-legalistic minds it is not exactly clear from the text of the agreement that a distinction was intended between *teams* having contact with South Africans, and individuals doing so. In England, at least, individuals have not been penalised for playing and coaching in the Republic, but, as already noted, the team which went on the sponsored tour of 1982 received a three-year ban from all of England's representative cricket. The Sri Lankans and West Indians who followed were effectively banned for life. As in Australia, so in South Africa, the men of commerce will soon take over from the men of cricket if the members of the International Cricket Conference do not soon follow up the recommendation of the

ICC fact-finding delegation of 1979 to send a strong, multi-racial international side to South Africa.

Even the most determined political opponents of South Africa would not necessarily reject such an idea. One such, Jill Wentzel, writing in a publication of the organisation Black Sash, which seeks to defeat apartheid through non-violent means, said:

> ' ... The all-or-nothing tactic governing current boycott policy has created a situation of stalemate, which classically drives people to seek strong-arm and unconstructive solutions – in this case, bribery of international sportsmen ...
>
> 'The current situation is dead, providing victory to no one, semi-defeat to everyone ...
>
> 'Overall the sports boycott put the South African political situation and the nature of apartheid on to the agenda of ordinary people overseas who were immediately able to relate to it within a field in which they had tremendous interest. In its early phase, the sports boycott succeeded dramatically in encouraging sportsmen to try to move away from sports apartheid. In its present all-or-nothing form it is an almost daily reminder to white South Africans that they are perceived by all the world to be wicked. Thinking people of all races, however, might at least ponder the sterility of the present situation. Even if there do not seem to be any immediate solutions, human rights organisations like Black Sash are surely duty-bound to think carefully about tactics which reject gradual reform and disable our society from changing itself non-violently.'

I was agreeably surprised when I visited South Africa early in 1984 to see the changes which had already taken place in the twenty years since my only previous first-hand experience of the country. I understood the force of Hassan Howa's arguments during an interesting discussion at his comfortable home in Cape Town, but I was more convinced by the statement of an Indian cricket official in Johannesburg – 'Our foot is in the door, now we must keep pushing' – than by Mr Howa's all-or-nothing approach. His is a brave, unselfish, but stubborn policy, the logical conclusion of which is violence.

For both political and cricketing reasons, therefore, there is a case for responding now to the ever more urgent pleas from South African cricketers and administrators to show tangible recognition of the changes they have fought for and achieved.

NINE

Cricket:
an Expanding World

The possibility of Africans taking up the game in large numbers in the southern tip of that vast continent was mentioned in the last chapter. Cricket, in fact, is played in what many might consider the strangest places. To name a few: Abu Dhabi, Bordeaux, Corfu, Denmark, Egypt, Finland, Gibraltar, Hong Kong, Israel, Jammu, Kenya, Lord Howe Island, Mauritius, New Caledonia, Osnabruck, Portugal, Riyadh, Samoa, Tanzania, Uganda, Varese, Winnipeg, Yokohama and Zambia.

The British, of course, were responsible for sowing the seeds of the game in most, if not all, of these places. In many of them the ground on which it has flowered is still thorny, and in need of greater care. But as the role of Britain has shrunk in world affairs, so, alas, has the influence of MCC, the traditional missionary of cricket.

Cricket in faraway places, even when the boats came in with troops or traders much more often than they do today, has always depended largely on voluntary enthusiasts. They are still active, still mainly English, but there has been a growing awareness in the last twenty years of the need to replace MCC's global role. This feeling received tangible expression in 1965 when, due mainly to the inspiration of S. C. Griffith, the Test-playing countries, who until then had been the only members of the International (formerly Imperial) Cricket Conference, invited three other countries to join them as 'associate members'. The pioneers were Ceylon (Sri Lanka), Fiji and the United States. Ceylon were represented by Gamini Goonesena, the Cambridge blue, Fiji by Philip Snow, and the USA by John I. Marder.

The new members were positively encouraged to give their views, in the annual meeting at Lord's, on all matters other than Test cricket. A coaching fund was set up with each of the major countries taking on responsibility for the lesser lights within their own sphere of influence. England, for example, is responsible for European countries and Canada; Australia for Malaysia and Papua New Guinea; West Indies for Bermuda; New Zealand for Fiji, and so on. Some countries have done more for their 'planets' than others, and there is a strong feeling that even more could be done to spread the gospel. Proper coaching, better facilities, and visits by leading players are all badly needed. Cricket, after all, is a complicated game, difficult to learn, requiring more time, more expertise and more specialist equipment than many other sports.

Since 1965 several more of the minor cricket countries have become associate members of the ICC. In order of election, they are: Bermuda, Denmark, East Africa and Holland (1966), Malaysia (1967), Canada (1968), Gibraltar and Hong Kong (1969), Papua New Guinea (1973), Argentina, Israel and Singapore (1974), West Africa (1976), Bangladesh (1978), and Zimbabwe and Kenya (1981).

In 1982 the associate members set up their own association to represent their interests, with Philip Snow, brother of C. P. (Lord) Snow, as chairman. He has been involved with the development of the minor cricketing powers since becoming Fiji's ICC representative from the outset in 1965. For many years a District Commissioner in the Fijian Islands, he led a very successful tour to New Zealand in 1948 and was instrumental in arranging the short visit of the England team to Fiji early in 1984 when Bob Willis's touring team was en route to New Zealand. The visit meant a great deal to cricket followers in Fiji who, with no television, had in most cases never seen the Bothams and Gowers of whom they read in their papers.

In the past there has been a somewhat shaming reluctance on the part of all the Test-playing countries, though England are least to blame, in fostering the needs of the smaller cricket countries by visits such as these and by loaning coaches and equipment. If growth in the smaller nations is to be maintained, or indeed if cricket is to survive at all, encouragement at schools level is crucial. This requires not just a willingness to help in monetary terms, or by providing either temporary or permanent coaches, but also help on a diplomatic level, since in many countries governments must be persuaded to lend their own resources to cricket education in schools. The Israelis, for example, have recognised the character-building virtues of cricket and the game has therefore received some official encouragement, though conditions for cricket in this arid land could hardly be worse.

The latter is true also of the nations at the other end of the political and religious divide, the Arab countries of the Middle East. There, since the oil and gas boom, cricket has flourished in recent years due to the influx of British businessmen and, even more significantly, of thousands of immigrant workers from Pakistan and India. Over fifty-five clubs now play regular weekend and some midweek cricket in Dubai and Sharjah alone, two of the small but important states which make up the United Arab Emirates. As yet the game has not attracted the official patronage of the ruling family, whose passions are racing and soccer. But millionaire Abdul Rahman Bukhatir has paid for the development of a superb cricket stadium at Sharjah, where a grass outfield miraculously flourishes in the middle of the desert. Several big matches have been held for Indian and Pakistani beneficiaries while the 1982–83 England touring team took on Pakistan there in an unofficial game on their way home from Australia. In 1984 Sharjah also staged the first Asian Cup, a series of limited-overs games between India, Pakistan, Sri Lanka and Bangladesh.

No such lavish patronage is available in Saudi Arabia, but wherever cricket is played enthusiasm counts for more than money. Some fifteen hundred cricketers play in leagues and a knockout tournament in Riyadh, Jeddah and Al Khobarand. In 1982 a cricket clinic was opened at the British School in Riyadh with two nets: and equipment worth £1200 was given to the local cricket association by a Welsh firm, thanks to the perseverance of one enthusiast, Chris Syer. An exhibition match was played before the King's son, Prince Feisal Bin Fahad.

Closer to home, there is still evidence of cricket's potential for creating enjoyable recreation and at the same time, in the old but now unfashionable phrase, 'building bridges' between people of different beliefs. In Ireland, all through the troubles and tensions of recent years, the game has continued to flourish, not least amongst women and children, and more people now play the game in the north and south of Ireland than ever before. The current estimate is in excess of ten thousand, about a quarter of whom are from the Catholic south. The Secretary of the Irish Cricket Union, Derek Scott, says it is no longer surprising to see the game being played by boys against a lamp post in a Dublin street. Big matches in recent years – including the annual international against Scotland, and games against English counties in the Benson and Hedges Cup – have attracted crowds of four thousand. Women's cricket has developed from the eight teams playing in Leinster in 1976 to twenty-seven now competing throughout the island.

Irishmen – let alone the West Indian touring team concerned – will never forget the astounding victory in 1969 when the West Indies touring team was bowled out for 25 by Alec O'Riordan of the Old Belvedere club and Dougie Goodwin of Malahide. The wider world of cricket is full of such delightful surprises. In 1983, to give but one other example, England's women's team were flown over to the USA by British Airways to play in a match against the West Indies at a baseball stadium in New York. The promoter, Bert Smith, wrote afterwards to Rachael Heyhoe-Flint, the inspiration of English women's cricket, to say that the visit had been a catalyst for turning cricket into a spectator sport in America. Well, the game has been played there longer than it has in Australia, so who is to say Mr Smith's enthusiasm is misplaced?

For most, though, the ambition is simply to play for fun. For those with higher aspirations the recent example of Sri Lanka is both an inspiration and a warning. The game in Ceylon dates from the formation of the first club at Colombo in 1832. By 1882 the first of many touring teams from England and Australia was calling in for a game as a break in the long sea journey. And in more recent years air travel enabled the Sri Lankan players, whose skill is based on a long tradition of cricket as the main sport in the schools, to test their abilities more often against the other Asian cricket countries. Officials in Pakistan, A. H. Kardar in particular, were particularly helpful.

In 1981 Sri Lanka was elevated to full membership of the ICC and played the inaugural Test against England in 1982. They were by no means outplayed, at least for the first two days of the game, but the lack of experience in anything other than one-day cricket has prevented the Sri Lankans, so far, from developing the immense ability of many of their players into a match-winning Test team.

TEN

Player Behaviour

Young people need heroes. They are the men, or women, on whom they model themselves. I shall never forget a cartoon in *The Cricketer* soon after Gary Sobers had joined Nottingham-shire depicting scores of schoolboys walking into the school yard with knees flicking and bodies leaning forward like the great man walking out to bat. Imitation is the sincerest form of flattery; hence the responsibility of the leading cricketers who are the heroes of their day is immense. Indeed, in the age of television it is all the greater – which only makes more sad the occasional lapses which have demeaned the game in recent years.

Many of these had their origin in the hyped-up version of cricket played by Packer's World Series cricketers in the two years between 1977 and 1979. In order to drum up publicity and television interest, the organisers of WSC encouraged such things as open discussion of prize-money, obtrusive advertis-ing, showbiz style playing to the gallery, and gamesmanship. Cricket was presented to its 'new' public in Australia not as a subtle, profound and skilful exercise, but as a game of blood and thunder played by larger than life characters in coloured clothes. The commentators on Channel Nine were, perhaps unwittingly, a part of the act, or the sales team, often building up mediocre performances into something superlative – and, often, failing to criticise when a player made a public exhibi-tion of his bad temper.

The selling of cricket to Australians since the Australian Board ensured peace by granting a ten-year marketing con-tract to PBL will be briefly discussed in Chapter Twelve. It is pertinent here, however, to make the point that the company has remained extremely aggressive – both in its marketing and in its positive encouragement of attitudes of hostility from players and spectators alike. In 1982, for instance, the forthcoming Ashes series was advertised on commercial television by a film showing archetypal 'Poms' giving their opinion that the Aussies had no chance of winning back the Ashes. 'Wait till Botham gets hold of your lot, he'll rip 'em apart'; 'Dennis Lillee is over the top'; 'We'll trounce the blighters'; 'Marsh is not the best wicket-keeper in the world but he must be nearly the oldest', are just a few examples.

Since this was the first series in which use was made of a giant television screen erected at the Melbourne Cricket Ground, it was asking for trouble, in my view, to incite the baser passions of the spectators beforehand by means of this film. British football has suffered immeasurable damage from spectator hooliganism and it would be tragic if people stopped going to cricket matches because they feared for life and limb. In the event, the 1982–83 series was relatively incident-free, apart from one calamity when the likeable West Australian fast bowler, Terry Alderman, unwisely tried to tackle an invading spectator and damaged his shoulder so badly that he missed the remainder of the season. It took him well over a year to re-establish himself. By now, however, the players were aware of the dangers. In Australia, as we have seen, they had felt it necessary to produce a player's code of conduct with fines applied by a special tribunal if the code was transgressed. In England the county cricketers resolved at a meeting of the Cricketers' Association to eliminate gamesmanship, dissent and 'unfair practices'.

For many, the realisation that something needed to be done had come too late, especially for those in Australia who knew that toughness and determination to win were not synonymous with gamesmanship and winning at all costs. To prove this, I publish below an extract from letters received from two Australians tired of the controversy and rancour which reached its peak in Australian cricket in 1980–81 and the following season, which saw the notorious argument on the pitch during which Lillee kicked the Pakistan captain, Javed Miandad.

The previous season Greg Chappell was involved in two incidents, first when failing to walk when it was obvious to all except the two umpires, who were looking for possible run-outs, that he had been caught in the deep by the New Zealander Martin Snedden, and the second when Chappell instructed his younger brother, Trevor, to bowl an underarm sneak when New Zealand needed six runs off the last ball to tie the third final of the one-day triangular tournament and thus share the substantial prize money. In the same season the Indian captain, Sunil Gavaskar, was so incensed when given out lbw in a Test that he told his partner to accompany him off the field: in his anger he saw no point in going on with the game.

The first letter was written on the last day of the same Test by Bob Strevens of Swan Hill, Victoria, and sent to me at *The Cricketer* with a view to possible publication:

> 'The whole season can be summed up in the word "unpleasant". I cannot recall a match in which there was not a confrontation of some kind either on or off the field. One has to be a super optimist to believe that the future holds anything different for Australian cricket. In short: the flesh is willing but the spirit is weak.
>
> 'A game it ain't. For one thing the season has been saturated with cricket, most of it played for large amounts of cash with minor portions of sportsmanship. On a scale of 10 I'd give it a rating of 2 due simply because it retained the name of cricket. The resemblance was coincidental.
>
> 'Obviously there was some good technical stuff. The Australians have, in the main, been vastly superior over-all, and, when at times they've looked like slipping, most close decisions have gone their way. This of course happens and you can't blame the lucky ones.

It's your turn next week. What you can blame is the appalling pressure put upon the umpires by the players. (And the instant replay.) The umpires here are not full-time. Compared with his English counterpart he is, or seems to be, incapable of dealing with the tantrums of the "top bananas" of any side. The cash being played for is enormous as you will have read and given the likelihood that out of the twenty-two players in each bonanza there will be several who would stop at very little to get their share of the gravy, it is not surprising that the umpires are under such pressure and make so many mistakes. Not only the players apply the pressure. Think of the crowds. You've only seen the MCG on TV. See it in Glorious Living Colour and hear the unbelievable roar of the Outer and then imagine you're an umpire listening for a snick. Then you'll know why you need to be stupid to put on a white coat. (Another black day yesterday. The Gavaskar lbw and more headlines. You will know all about it before you get this so I will not elaborate. What will today bring? Australia 3 for 24 chasing 143. I understand the umpires were in church all night praying for rain.)

'So what of the future? As sick as the game is here there is too much money at the bedside to start speaking of funerals. What will happen, I think, as cricket becomes more and more dependent on TV for its income, the razzamatazz will be increased and the rules (Laws? What Laws?) will be decided by the TV producer.

'How all this will affect the relationships of the teams on future tours will be nothing if not exciting. Australia in England this year. England and West Indies in Australia at the end of this year. The mind boggles!

'Knowing the English (and I know them better now after being in this country for over twenty years than I ever did during the forty odd I lived with them), they will object to most changes and it will be on again *ad nauseam*.

'It would be nice to think that things will cool down this year. It will probably get a lot worse before it gets better. Possibly the First Cricket Punch-up (at Test match level of course) will be necessary before the cricketing boards do something. The ACB produced a code of "Players' Behaviour" and then apparently forgot all about it. Not even a finger wagging and not a single fine in a very good year for fines. The elder statesmen of Australian cricket such as McGilvray and Hassett are not amused and are trying to put this right. Good luck to them.

'But enough of the whingeing. Perhaps cricket is not all that important in the scheme of things. On the other hand maybe it, and *not* golf is the sole reason we are here. Whatever – I think I have come to terms with the "Knew Kricket" and watch it on TV as a sort of sporting western. Not too many good guys but no shortage of bad guys. Plenty of shoot-outs at twenty-two yards and boy, don't them crazy cowhands in them fancy duds give those sheriffs a time of it!

'Speaking of good guys I always picked Greg Chappell as one. Not any more. You know how it is from our side of the TV. We don't know the players personally, so we can only form an opinion of them by their TV performances. Chappell to date was a good guy. Nothing really snow white about the man but then nothing really black. In theatrical terms he "underplayed". No histrionics. No ham. Impassive and, to me, very impressive, until last weekend. It wasn't so much the underarm that earned him my black hat award. That was a childish spur of the moment decision (with the odd thought about the cash angle) and I can think of several recent captains who could have done the same and, like Chappell, regretted it later. What made him a bad guy was refusing to walk when he'd been caught by Snedden.

'He had time to think about that, and it epitomises the present day attitude of, in effect, calling a fellow professional a liar when the catch was claimed. You may remember the umpires were busily engaged looking for one short and not watching the ball as it sailed into the outfield! That action lost me and I freely admit a smile of great satisfaction when the mighty one was bowled first ball in the second innings of the present Test match.

'The fuss over here was considerable. For just one day. Most of the letters condemning him probably came from New Zealanders or English migrants anyway and it was no surprise to find that within a couple of days he was as great a hero as ever. (I don't doubt the British press didn't so quickly forgive and they don't forget very quickly do they?) The press here started off with a big blast but he only had to get a big score (which he duly did next match) for all to be forgiven. Most of the writers came up with something on the lines of: "Greg Chappell was forgiven yesterday when he answered his critics with a flawless innings . . ." etc, etc. As if anybody had criticised his ability. No. Along with the other bad guys of Aussie cricket, Chappell will have to help a lot of little old umpires across the street before he gets a white hat from this viewer. And hell! it's not that I'm running short.

'Last day of the season today. In just under an hour the Aussies will start their chase although I feel it will be mostly a crawl. The TV gang of six: Benaud, Tyson, Greig, Ian Chappell, Bill Lawry and Stackpole will add their colourless commentaries and criticise and criticise and criticise. Captains all and don't they let you know it. Some think they are great but then commentators are a matter of taste and I was spoilt many years ago.

'(Back to finish this after watching the Indians finish

Australia. A great victory indeed and, permitting myself a rather nasty smirk, very well deserved!)'

The second letter was part of an appeal sent to several
people, including myself, on 31 August, 1982, by John Hurley,
from Carngham in Victoria, who correctly pointed out that 'a
small minority of our cricketers, by their undignified behaviour, have captured the attention of the world press'. By
circulating his views Mr Hurley hoped to start a groundswell
of public opinion which would convince the Australian
Cricket Board that the dignity of Australian cricket was being
challenged. He reserved his severest strictures for Dennis
Lillee, his country's greatest fast bowler, whose belligerent
showmanship was not appreciated by everyone:

> 'Because of its recent record we can expect no relief
> from the Australian Cricket Board. We were sold to
> the Packer interests for a mess of potage and what a
> mess it has turned out to be. Maybe there was some
> commercial practicality in this latter exercise, I don't
> profess to know, but the subsequent dealings of the
> Board with the outlandish behaviour of Mr Lillee give
> one little confidence that they are aware of the ex-
> pectations of most members of the public of accept-
> able behaviour, by those representing this country in
> cricket.
>   'I challenge the Board to explain, in the simplest
> terms, its motives in permitting some of our leading
> cricketers to represent our country when they have
> kicked opposing players, sworn at umpires, authorised
> underarm bowling, heckled the opposing team, un-
> dressed on the cricket field, etc, etc, not to mention
> positively competing with established cricket.
>   'To think that the dignity of a game which has
> captured the imagination of generation after genera-
> tion the world over of all creeds and colours, a game,
> or better still, a way of life, played on hastily prepared

pitches in the Lebanon by Australian soldiers preparatory to their despatch to the Battle of Alamein, and on similarly prepared strips on the Atherton Tablelands en route to the jungles of New Guinea, should become a commercial plaything is an affront that not only cricket but our culture cannot withstand.'

Mr Hurley made his points well. Slow, gracious and kind are no longer words in the vocabulary of Australian first-class cricket. The 1982–83 Ashes series passed without serious incident, other than the Alderman injury, largely through the strength of character of the England captain, Bob Willis, who resolutely refused to 'whinge' despite often intense provocation. But there was more trouble between the Australian and New Zealand teams which reached the finals, again, of the triangular limited-overs tournament. Geoff Howarth, the New Zealand captain, said that he would complain to the Australian Board about the amount of swearing, 'sledging' (abuse of the batsman), and unchecked short-pitched fast bowling to which his team had been subjected. At the same time, Rodney Marsh and Kim Hughes both cheerfully admitted to breaches of the spirit of cricket: Marsh by deliberately kicking the ball out of a fielder's way to avoid being run out, and Hughes by telling his fast bowler, Rodney Hogg, to take as long as possible over bowling the forty-ninth over of the New Zealand innings so as to prevent the opposition receiving their full quota in the time available – not that Hughes was alone in using that sort of gamesmanship.

There has, however, been all too little effort by umpires in Australia and, more important, by the Australian Cricket Board, to take a firm line when their players transgress in this way. In 1979–80, when Lillee held up a Test for ten minutes after the umpires had told him to change his aluminium bat for a wooden one, he was merely warned about his behaviour by the Board. Again, when he kicked Javed Miandad out of pique after the latter, a provocative character himself, had scored a run off his bowling, and Lillee had tried to block his path, the punishment hardly fitted the crime: Lillee was suspended for two one-day internationals.

Lillee remained a rebel to the last. After his retirement from Test cricket in 1984, he insisted on taking a drinks break during a Sheffield Shield match, defying the orders of the umpires not to do so. It took a decision by a High Court Judge to uphold the umpires' decision. 'Unless it is obeyed', said the Judge, 'cricket would be unplayable.' It was sad to think that many people breathed a sigh of relief when Lillee announced his retirement. He was a great cricketer who behaved too often like a spoiled child.

Commenting on the accusations by Howarth, Greg Chappell, who, despite the incidents against New Zealand, had been involved in far fewer moments of uncouth behaviour than his elder brother, Ian, said: 'I am not trying to condone the fact that we occasionally swear on the field, that we are aggressive and that we have been accused of being arrogant. I think we probably have been, but no more arrogant than the England side of 1970–71 or the West Indian teams we have played in recent years.' Chappell and Marsh joined Lillee in retirement after the 1983–84 season. It was very much the end of an era.

It would certainly be quite wrong to give the impression that Australia has had a monopoly of bad behaviour on the field, just as it would be wrong to suggest that such behaviour is typical, for, on the whole, it is not. In *all* countries where cricket has been played for high financial stakes in recent years there has been plenty of cause for anxiety about the game's traditional belief (however often it has been broken in the past) in sportsmanship and fair play.

Three West Indian fast bowlers were involved in disgraceful scenes at the beginning and end of 1980 which revealed how alarmingly easily cricketers can break under the pressure of modern international cricket. Tired after a successful and lucrative tour of Australia, Clive Lloyd's team went on to New Zealand, perhaps spoilt by their recent success and expecting an easy ride. When things started to go against them, discipline was found to be sadly lacking. During New Zealand's victory in the First Test, Michael Holding kicked down the stumps in fury after John Parker had been given not out following a confident 'caught behind' appeal. Then, after another appeal had been turned down in the Second Test at Christchurch, Colin Croft deliberately barged into umpire Goodall as he ran up to bowl a ball. On the same day the team had appeared 12 minutes late after tea, having at one point sent a message to say that they would not come out if Mr Goodall remained as umpire. It later transpired that several senior West Indians had been in favour of abandoning the tour there and then, and that evening they duly left their dressing-room bare. But strong words of sanity from Jeff Stollmeyer in Trinidad to the tour manager, Willie Rodriguez, who appeared to have little control over his players, enabled the cricketers to see sense and play on to the finish of a very unhappy tour.

At the end of 1980 there was a potentially even worse incident when Sylvester Clarke, being pelted by oranges whilst fielding on the boundary during a Test in Multan (as many a cricketer in the Orient has been pelted before) lost his temper. In a moment of madness, he threw a brick into the crowd, badly injuring a spectator. If he had killed the unfortunate student concerned he would, presumably, have faced a charge of manslaughter, if not of murder.

Tempers also boiled over in a big match in South Africa in 1982. Before a full house at the Wanderers Ground in Johannesburg, and on television, Vintcent Van der Bijl (the giant fast-medium bowler who had much to do with Middlesex's success in the County Championship in the year he played for them, 1980), ran out Allan Lamb when there was no question of Lamb attempting a run. His partner, Kuiper, had played the ball back to the bowler and started to signal for another bat. Lamb was a little out of his crease when Van der Bijl, having started back towards his mark with the ball, suddenly turned and threw down the stumps. Later in the match, Peter Kirsten, captaining Western Province, returned the compliment with a vengeance. Van der Bijl had survived a confident appeal for a snick to the wicket-keeper whereupon much discussion ensued amongst the fielders, a bad example of the increasing tendency in some countries to let the umpire know, by words or gestures of dissent, when the batsmen, bowlers or fielders reckon he has made a mistake. In the hiatus, Van der Bijl's partner, the Rhodesian Paddy Clift, walked up the pitch to discuss tactics. Kirsten promptly picked up a ball which ought to have been considered dead (it had long since left the wicket-keeper's gloves) and threw down Clift's wicket.

The late Alan Melville, the former South African and Sussex captain, who was watching the match, commented on Kirsten's action: 'I'm sure he would not have done it had there been no money at stake. But then we must realise that the whole spirit of the game has altered today because of money, and sportsmanship and chivalry have disappeared.'

Another former Test player, Athol Rowan, asked: 'What's happened to the wonderful spirit of cricket? In my day we played just as hard as these guys today – but we would never think of doing anything to offend the spirit of the game. We would never do anything unethical.'

The modern counter to that, perhaps, came in one of those advertisements for the big matches in Australia, in which Dennis Lillee faced the camera and said: 'Winning is what it is all about.'

There is nothing new in that sentiment. But, taken to extremes, as these examples prove, it sours the game and threatens its future.

A South African Sunday newspaper sports editor, writing in defence of the actions of Van der Bijl and Kirsten in the Datsun cup final incidents, claimed: 'The essence of sport is controversy.' The essence of a certain type of sports journalism, perhaps. But not of sport itself.

The *Oxford Dictionary* defines sports as 'amusement, diversion, fun'. Cricket, at all levels, would do well to remember that it is first and foremost still a sport. To those who say, no, at first-class level it is a business, the reply can only be that it will only succeed as a business if it is true to its spirit. Too much controversy will kill both the sport and the business.

ELEVEN

Umpires:
Pigs in the Middle

The late Arthur Fagg, a gifted and high-scoring batsman for Kent, and not unsuccessful in his five Tests for England, is reputed to have been asked by a disgruntled Australian batsman, Bill Lawry, why he had just given him out.

'Lbw,' was Fagg's reply as Lawry walked past him at the bowler's end, en route for the pavilion.

'Lbw?' said Lawry in disgust. 'But I hit the b....y ball.'

'I know,' said Fagg, 'that's why I gave you out caught behind.'

Not many umpires get the last word these days, and certainly not many in Test matches.

The same Arthur Fagg refused to umpire at the start of one day's play in the Edgbaston Test between England and West Indies in 1973, so incensed was he by the reaction of the captain, Rohan Kanhai, and some of the other West Indies players when Fagg had turned down an appeal against Geoff Boycott for a catch behind the wicket. That evening he had told reporters:

> 'I will ask Rohan Kanhai this morning whether he wants me to continue umpiring in this Test. If not, I'll pack up and they can get someone else. If they won't accept decisions, there is no point in carrying on. Why should I? I am nearly sixty. I don't have to live with this kind of pressure.
>
> 'I've had to live with it for two and a half hours out there. People don't realise how bad it has become. I don't enjoy umpiring Tests any more, nor

Sunday League matches. There is so much at stake.

'The players shout for things and when they don't get the decision, they react the way Kanhai reacted today. The game has changed, and not for the better. Umpires are under terrific pressure.

'The players have to learn to accept decisions, otherwise there is no point continuing. We are human, the same as everyone else, and we make mistakes, as players make mistakes. It doesn't matter whether it was out or not, it is the umpire's decision.

'Boycott signalled with his arm that the ball brushed his leg and looked at me for the decision. When players are trying it on, they don't look at you. I did not see any deviation.'

Arthur Fagg insisted that if he did not get an apology from Kanhai, he would leave the match. In fact the apology did not come until much later, but the difference between this incident and the one in New Zealand involving Clive Lloyd's team was that the manager, Esmond Kentish, took a firm hand, publicly expressing the confidence of the West Indies team in Arthur Fagg's umpiring and helping to persuade him to continue his duties after missing the first over the following morning.

Test umpires everywhere – indeed all umpires at all levels, for I have always maintained that most batsmen have as their motto 'If at first you don't succeed, blame it on the umpire' – will have both identified and sympathised with Fagg. Things have undoubtedly grown worse since, at the highest level, and a tour now seldom passes in any country without either the press or the players stirring up some controversy or other. Four groups of people are to blame for this deviation from one of the fundamental principles of the game, namely that the umpire's decision is final: they are the players, the umpires themselves, cricket reporters and those involved in television.

For as long as the BBC in England and the ABC in Australia were responsible for the coverage of Test cricket, there was a clear policy on the part both of producers and of commentators to play down any incident arising from a controversial umpiring decision. If a slow-motion replay of a decision was shown, it often exonerated the umpire in any case. If it did not, the commentators would merely restrict themselves to some all-embracing statement such as 'that looked close'. After all, anyone who has played cricket knows how devilish hard the umpire's job is, and how much harder still when a television camera is scrutinising every decision. A similar policy has been pursued for radio commentaries: no criticism given of an umpire's decision on the field (those on bad light or wet grounds perhaps leave more room for fair discussion).

Since the coming of Channel Nine to the televising of Australian cricket, however, more cameras and more commentators have been involved and the treatment of umpires has been altogether less reticent. No doubt the policy can be defended on the grounds that if players can be criticised, why should not umpires be too? They are, after all, in England at least, professionals, and, since the Packer revolution, they have been much better paid for their exacting job. But it is a patent absurdity that the slow-motion replay should be available to millions of viewers when a difficult decision has had to be made, yet not to the umpires who have to pronounce irrevocable judgment. There is no doubt that the time has come, in important televised matches such as Test and one-day internationals, for a third official to be involved. Preferably he should be a qualified umpire, or possibly an experienced and respected match 'referee', neutral to and acceptable to both sides, and he should watch a monitor throughout the game so as to be able to give swift judgment if ever the umpires in the middle require a second opinion. He would not be needed very often, but for run-out and stumping decisions in particular the slow-motion replay can actually prove something. In these cases his opinion should be sought.

One should not lightly toss away the fact that umpiring itself is not always of the highest standard. The steadily more persistent calls for neutral umpires in Test matches often overlook the fact that you gain nothing by neutrality except the elimination of the possibility that a bad decision has been made because it favoured the home side. If, for example, a universally respected official like Harold Bird of England were to be replaced by an umpire from overseas during a series of Tests in England, the chances are that the players of both sides would be condemned to judgment by someone less competent. On the whole, despite some recent lapses, the umpires who stand in English county cricket are the best in the world – both because most of them have played the game at a high level and because they do the job almost every day for five months.

It would also be very expensive to pay for the travel, board and fees of an international panel of umpires, which would have to be quite large to cater for the increasing number of Tests played round the globe in the English close season.

Nevertheless, one can see some point in captains and managers reporting secretly at the end of each tour on the worth of the umpires chosen to officiate in the big games, leading to the development of a panel of men (or even of women if they were good enough) who could stand both at home and, by invitation of the home authority, overseas too whenever they were available.

For some time touring sides have had the option of quietly refusing an umpire for a big match, something normally done before the names of the officials have been announced, to avoid embarrassment. England and India unfortunately broke this rule in 1981–82, when England made it known that they had objected to the appointment of Mohammad Ghouse for the Third Test in Delhi, while in England the following summer the Pakistanis objected to David Constant. This might well have been an unfortunate retaliatory gesture.

In one of his dispatches to *The Cricketer* during England's tour of Australia in 1982–83, Vic Marks wrote: 'The team was also urged to improve its appealing, an area in which the Australians are undoubtedly superior. When appealing the Australians make a statement: we ask a question.'

Here was an innocent admission from an honest man that gamesmanship has become an accepted tactic in international cricket. Or is 'gamesmanship' not too euphemistic a term to use for appealing for a catch off bat and pad, when fielders and bowlers know the batsman has not touched the ball? Is this not cheating? If so, most Test teams of recent years are guilty of it; not all the time, but often enough when the pressure is on. As an English umpire said to me of the England and New Zealand sides in 1983: 'They are two very nice sides. Cheats, mind you, but nice cheats.'

In general, cricketers will reap what they sow. Frivolous appeals, which have become all too frequent in Test cricket over the last ten years in particular, merely increase the chance of umpiring mistakes. In a vicious circle, mistakes then lead to player histrionics – except where captains firmly make it team policy not to show dissent, as England under Willis have done. Histrionics, either subtle, as in the case of a concentrated study of the bat by the condemned batsman as he walks out after being adjudged lbw, or obvious, as in the case of throwing up the arms and glaring at the umpire in amazement, merely disturb the umpire's confidence and concentration. They also lead to instant inquests on the television and an 'in-depth probe' in the popular press the next morning. Often, nowadays, certain newspapers have two reporters at a Test match, one to report the cricket and another to analyse anything remarkable, or anything controversial, that arises.

Dedicated, experienced and carefully selected umpires, preferably former players of at least first-class standard; responsible captains and managers; disciplined players; and sympathetic commentators and journalists are the answer to the problem.

If common sense does not prevail, there will inevitably be a further decline, leading to the empowering of umpires with punishments they do not want. Gerry Gomez, the former West Indies Test all-rounder, who stood as umpire in one Test and is President of the West Indian Umpires Association, has already suggested that umpires should have the power to send players off the field for bad behaviour, either for a short cooling-off period in an ice-hockey style 'sin-bin', or for the match. But cricket does not want its McEnroes. The game is appealing enough without the kind of publicity they attract. Whoever said that all publicity is good was wrong: bad publicity is, in the end, self-defeating.

TWELVE

Marketing the Game

The impeccable image of professional golf, not the mass hysteria of soccer, is the one which players and promoters in cricket must work towards. It is, after all, no accident that golfing galleries are increasing whilst soccer crowds are declining. Instead of presenting their 'aggro awards', as Channel Nine did in 1982–83, packaging a series of occasional moments of bad temper during the season, surely they should have been emphasising the beauty, grace and chivalry of cricket. This is still, for all the exceptions which prove the rule, its true image: and, I believe, what the majority of cricket fans want from their game.

Many things in modern cricket bear witness to this true image. The beauty, for example, of Michael Holding's gazelle-like approach to the stumps; the grace of a drive by David Gower or Greg Chappell; or the chivalry in defeat after the 1983 World Cup final of Viv Richards, the greatest batsman in the world. Smilingly, he signed autographs in the darkness outside Lord's though he knew that if he had gone on batting in the way that he had been in his short stay at the crease a few hours earlier, even for half an hour longer, his side must have won. If marketing is now accepted as necessary if cricket is to develop its share of the 'leisure' market, one hopes that these genuine selling points will be used. It is true of any business, however, that the attractions of the product need constantly to be placed before the customer if he is to 'buy' on a regular basis, a fundamental commercial principle which PBL Ltd in Australia have stressed to the Australian Cricket Board since their 'marriage' in 1979.

In PBL's case, the marketing of cricket is bound up with the need to pull in viewers for their sister company, Channel Nine. More viewers means more advertisements and accordingly more profit for Channel Nine. For the first time, therefore, in cricket history (it having always been assumed in the past that, with the free and willing support of the media, the game would sell itself) PBL have set out to examine and exploit the cricket 'market'.

In Australia there is certainly more reason to do this than in some other countries where cricket is firmly established as a main summer sport from schooldays onwards. At the time of the last Australian census, the population was 13,548,467, of which 88.8 per cent were of European origin. As many as 2,718,855 had been born overseas, and immigration has grown apace since then. Of the immigrants in the last census, European countries other than the United Kingdom accounted for slightly more of the immigrants than those from Britain. One may safely assume that only the tiniest handful of these non-British immigrants were born and brought up in a tradition of cricket. A generation further back, 1,319,856 of the Australian-born population of 10,829,661 (at the time of the last census) were born overseas. So for them, too, cricket was likely to be an alien game to be accepted and adopted, or ignored and rejected, as they saw fit.

Many of these immigrants, or second-generation Australians, were attracted by the novelty of World Series Cricket matches, which were deliberately sold to them via Channel Nine as something new, colourful and exciting. To these people the tradition of the Ashes meant nothing. In a Freudian slip in February 1979, Kerry Packer said: 'It has probably been one of the most successful launches of a new sport ever seen.'

In many ways, World Series Cricket was presented as a *new* sport, catering for the Americanised tastes of modern Australian society. From the name 'World Series' to the coloured clothes, night-time play and hyped-up presentation, it was clearly influenced by American baseball. Since the peace, PBL Ltd have had to try to marry the reliable core of supporters for traditional cricket with the new audience they believed they had created, not that all of it was 'new' by any means. There have always been plenty of young people amongst cricket crowds in Australia.

But there is no doubting the upward trend in the number of spectators for the triangular series of one-day matches held each Australian season since 1979–80. The average attendance for these games in that season, when England and West Indies were the visitors, was 18,510. By the time of the England and New Zealand visits in 1982–83, the average had grown to 32,440 per international – well in excess of the capacity of England's largest ground, Lord's! To some extent this reflected the success of the sophisticated marketing now applied to Australian cricket. A sample survey is taken each Australian winter about the cricket programme for the forthcoming summer, when questions are put about the attractiveness of the touring teams, the price of tickets, the views on various Australian players, and so on. Before Pakistan's visit for five Tests in 1983–84, PBL were faced with a problem. The poll had shown that only Imran Khan was an instantly recognisable name and face amongst the visiting team, and that Pakistan (despite their recent successes) were not considered likely by the man in the street to extend seriously such players as Lillee, Lawson and Marsh. Accordingly, Lynton Taylor, the managing director of PBL, designed an advertising campaign with the aim of building up the Pakistan team as a threat, forcing the names of their outstanding players down the public throat. In an average year, Mr Taylor believes that such research, and consequential campaigns, can raise by some twenty per cent the size of the crowds who would otherwise go to watch. Illogically, Mr Taylor believes the 'persuasion percentage' to be even higher in an Ashes series.

Whether such marketing research techniques can be successfully applied to arrest the declining trend in spectators for competitions like the County Championship and the Sheffield Shield is a pertinent point. As we have seen, the emphasis on international cricket seriously detracts from these essential tournaments, the training-ground for future Test cricketers. Australian society, being very media-orientated, is more easily exploited by advertisers than, for example, the West Indian islands, where attendance at cricket matches has always been entirely reflective of what the public thinks of the players on view, and is often affected by sudden social whim, such as the 'boycotting' of the Trinidad Test in 1981 because Deryck Murray, Trinidad's captain, had been dropped from the Test team. West Indians are much more aware of the cost of watching cricket than another poor nation, India. Even in the subcontinent there have been warning signs that the idolatry of cricketers and full houses for all big matches are not to be relied upon for ever.

Responsible marketing, therefore, undoubtedly has a role to play in maintaining the attractiveness of first-class cricket. But in the end it is the quality of the players, and the entertainment they provide, which really matters.

THIRTEEN

TV or not TV?

The first cricket match to be televised was the Lord's Test of 1938 – an auspicious start, since Wally Hammond played one of his greatest innings and Don Bradman also scored a century. (Since he scored one in each Test in which he batted in that series there was a fair chance that the viewers would be lucky!) However, it was not until 1959 that extensive portions of Test matches were allowed to be shown, so it is in the last twenty years or so that the influence of television on the game has been most profound.

The power of 'the box' cannot be overestimated. We have seen what happened when a powerful television magnate decided he wanted the game for his commercial channel in Australia. In Britain recently we have witnessed two 'static' sports, snooker and darts, which none but a few diehard enthusiasts would ever have dreamed of as spectator sports, suddenly becoming popular with millions following them on television.

Every three years, the Test and County Cricket Board indulges in an exercise in brinksmanship as its members try to determine what the Corporation should pay for the privilege of televising first-class cricket. On one hand the Board knows that cricket on television is immensely popular with viewers and also a relatively cheap form of television; on the other, the members know that ITV have never seriously challenged the BBC (except on one occasion in the 1960s when London Weekend Television, then associated with the soccer entrepreneur, Jimmy Hill, tried to compete for part of the contract) and that it will be some time before cable television provides a viable alternative to a BBC monopoly. The Board cannot afford to lose the television coverage, both because of the income from television itself and because sponsoring companies would no longer be attracted if their major matches at least were not televised.

Cornhill's executives would be the first to agree with that. When they moved in to sponsor Test cricket in England from 1978 onwards the 'public awareness' of their company was two per cent. Five years later, when they cheerfully renewed their contract with the TCCB, seventeen per cent of the public knew all about Cornhill Insurance. Profits have reflected this new awareness, enabling the company to move from the second division to the first amongst the big insurance companies.

Everyone was happy. Test players and umpires got huge rises overnight, thus enabling them to match the salaries of those players who had rejected Test cricket in order to join Mr Packer. Indirectly, smaller rises filtered through to the average county cricketers through larger annual TCCB handouts. Cornhill paid the TCCB one million pounds for the first five years of their sponsorship. In 1982 they announced a three-year extension of the contract, worth £600,000 to the Board in 1983 and the same amount, adjusted upwards in line with inflation, in the following two seasons. In return, apart from press and radio coverage and the prestige which came from being linked to Test cricket, Cornhill have benefited from vastly more air-time exposure than any other sponsor of sport in Britain, as the following figures from 1981 indicate:

1. Cornhill Insurance Test
   Matches   166 hours 28 minutes
2. Embassy Snooker   72 hours 28 minutes
3. State Express Snooker   36 hours 20 minutes
4. John Player League   33 hours 47 minutes
5. NatWest Bank Trophy   26 hours 25 minutes
6. Prudential Assurance Cup   24 hours 25 minutes
7. Benson and Hedges Cup   20 hours 5 minutes

These figures were released by a company called Sportscan, who also revealed that television coverage of sport amounted to 1831 hours in 1981. Sport on television is very cheap, one reason why a quarter of the viewing hours on the BBC are now devoted to it, although it accounts for only thirteen per cent of the costs. An hour of sport costs approximately £17,000, compared with £142,000 for drama or £52,000 for light entertainment. Cricket, however, is one of the costliest sports to televise, and it would be even more so if the BBC had as many cameras in operation at a Test match as Channel Nine do in Australia, where each shot can be seen from almost every conceivable angle.

There is a strong feeling amongst cricket officials in England that the game was sold much too cheaply to the BBC in 1959 and thereafter, at a time when any sudden injection of income was welcome. How seriously television has affected the gates for big matches is difficult to say. In the case of the one-day finals at Lord's the answer is not at all. These games are always sell-outs, regardless of the fact that they are live on television for much of the day. But live television has undoubtedly kept many a spectator away in summers when the touring side has not captured the public imagination, or even simply because the weather on a particular day has been uncertain, cold or damp – days when an armchair seems much preferable to a hard seat and expensive beer and sandwiches.

On the other hand, television has inspired the initial interest of many youngsters. Classic matches, such as the England/Australia Test at Headingley in 1981, the Lord's draw between England and West Indies in 1963, Laker's Test at Old Trafford in 1956, gripped the interest of almost the entire nation, in a way that would not have been possible in the days before television.

The dangers arise when television becomes so important in the scheme of sport that events are actually built around television schedules. This has become true of athletics in Britain. I have no doubt it is also true of much sport in America. And in Australia there have been moments in the last few years when one has wondered if the power of television and commercial interests has not dissuaded the Australian Cricket Board from taking stronger disciplinary action against recalcitrant players. Perhaps it has even influenced selectors to choose 'popular' players, like Doug Walters (suddenly recalled after apparently being discarded) or David Hookes.

Pay-as-you-view television, though not recommended by the Hunt Report on cable television, could become a major new source of income for cricket. Two million people – an audience often achieved by televised Test cricket – paying 20p each to watch a day's play could bring in £400,000 a day, of which cricket itself would no doubt be the main beneficiary.

Such sums are by no means pipe-dreams. After all, in 1981 the TCCB made £170,000 out of the twenty million calls made to British Telecom's scores service.

The most important thing of all is that the cricket authorities should not fall into the same trap as their counterparts in association football, who thought that recorded highlights would be better for the game than live matches. Viewers who once were prepared to go and watch Darlington play Aldershot on a Saturday afternoon were gradually spoiled by a diet of the best international, first division and European football, skimped of all its dull moments and presented as a glossy, all-action package. Anyone who has seen a day's Test cricket and then watched the half-hour or less of highlights in the evening will know how deceptive the highlights can be, no matter how sympathetically they are edited.

FOURTEEN

Sponsorship

Sponsorship of a sort is as old, almost, as organised cricket. The keen cricketing landowners of the eighteenth century would happily employ anyone likely to win them prestige – and sometimes the share of a generous purse – in challenge matches against rival aristocratic enthusiasts of the game.

Private patrons continued to support cricket until, in the second half of the nineteenth century, county clubs began to organise themselves for regular competition and the era of international cricket began. The first commercial sponsors were the catering firm, Spiers and Pond, who, having failed to secure Charles Dickens for a tour of lectures and readings, instead sponsored the first team of English professionals to tour Australia. They made a handsome profit, and sponsors ever since have found the fashionable game of cricket a useful means of advertising themselves, and a valuable way to improve their 'image' by associating their name with something considered honourable and prestigious. Only in the two decades under review has cricket, both amateur and professional, actually gone looking for commercial sponsorship. In that time it has become acceptable for almost every competition in all classes of cricket to receive some financial support from somebody.

The catalyst was the Gillette Cup. The decline in cricket's finances in the 1950s came at a time when, under influence from the other side of the Atlantic, the science (or is it the art?) of marketing and advertising was becoming much more sophisticated. There were other ways to sell things than by advertisements in the press or over the air. Sponsorship of cricket appealed especially to large firms who needed not so much a direct hard sell as to keep their name in the public eye, and to be seen to be supporting something traditional and worthwhile, as well as something popular and exciting.

It was observed in the last chapter that Cornhill Insurance found that fifteen per cent more of the United Kingdom population recognised their name and knew what it stood for as a result of their association with English Test cricket. Cornhill were one of several sponsors who in 1984 were underwriting first-class cricket in England to the tune of more than two million pounds. The oldest of the existing sponsors, John Player, led the way with a payment of £340,000, followed by Nat West Bank, who contributed £325,000. The newest sponsors, Texaco Oil, an American company, saw nothing incongruous in associating itself with cricket; it pumped in, so to speak, £275,000 for the privilege of succeeding the Prudential as sponsor of the one-day internationals – in this case only three games. Benson and Hedges, having negotiated earlier, perhaps had a better deal – £275,000 for a competition occupying regular space in the newspapers for the first two-thirds of the summer, together with some television coverage from the quarter-final stages on. Ironically the County Championship – without which Test matches and the various one-day competitions would be less attractive spectacles than they are, since many of the skills displayed therein have been taught and learned in the hard school of the Championship – lost its sponsor at the end of the 1983 season. In my view this was less the fault of the Championship itself, which still has daily coverage (a sponsor would call it 'exposure'), in the papers and on radio, but of those who advised Schweppes on how best to capitalise on their patronage of the oldest county competition. Dr Nigel Waite's *The management of sponsorship*, a detailed study of 106 companies in sixteen different industries, showed that whereas in 1971 sponsorship accounted for less than 2 per cent of the promotional budget, eight years later 40 per cent of those companies allocated more than 5 per cent. Of the reasons given for doing so, the most important was 'publicity in television, radio and press'; but the second most important (indeed in the case of 18 per cent of the firms the prime objective) was that it was a 'cost-effective way of entertaining important customers'. Cornhill Insurance found that in addition to their annual payment to the TCCB, they had to spend up to 75 per cent again on 'servicing the sponsorship', to cover such demands as fees to their highly professional agents, West Nally; entertaining; and promotional literature. Schweppes, on the other hand, failed, so far as one could tell, to use their sponsorship in this way and also seemed strangely reluctant to support their investment with secondary advertising and 'promotional back-up'.

On the whole, cricket has looked after its sponsors well, and vice versa. In one case, that of Gillette, the reason given for withdrawing after eighteen years was that people had begun to associate the name of Gillette more with cricket than with razor blades!

All sports sponsorships start with goodwill on both sides but as an independent report on sponsorship in cricket and football stated in May 1981:

'The middle men have become an essential link in the wealthy sponsorship chain . . . the sponsor who goes it alone may find he wastes his money which is then lost to the sport for the future . . . the total turnover handled by sport's middle men is around £250,000,000. For sponsorship is only one element . . . to it has to be added general promotion and merchandising of sport and individual performers, perimeter board advertising, and the lucrative area of star players' endorsements and personal appearances.'

This report, initially inspired by Trevor Bailey, warned of a 'circle of temptation' inherent in any cricket sponsorship. The players can begin to look on the sponsorship simply as a source of income for themselves, with scant regard to the needs of either the sport or the sponsor; the middle men may become too powerful, able to dictate to governing bodies, as IMG, Mark McCormack's organisation, does to golf – which special event is arranged, and which of their contracted players will appear in which event. The influence of PBL in Australian cricket has already been cited. It is equally tempting for sporting bodies to accept the highest bidder without thinking of the need to develop a sport in its own best long-term interests; gimmicks to please the new sponsor have been firmly resisted by the TCCB in England, but were eagerly accepted, initially at least, by the Australian Cricket Board.

There are temptations of the same kind for the sponsoring company, who may want to force unnecessary changes on the sport, or demand excessive 'free advertising' by pressing commentators for extra mentions and altering the placement of advertising boards. In Britain the BBC operate under strict guidelines as to what is and what is not acceptable. Nor, in my experience, has undue pressure ever been applied to either the BBC or the cricket authorities by the sponsors of English first-class cricket.

Indeed cricket has been very fortunate in its sponsors, who all have good reasons for 'giving away' their money, none entirely altruistic, except the Lord's Taverners, the cricketing charity which gives over £100,000 each year to the game at grass-roots level. Both the Nat West Bank and the Commercial Union insurance company, which sponsors several county youth competitions and batting and bowling awards for county cricketers under twenty-three, are less concerned with direct profits than with their 'overall image'. As a senior official of the Nat West Bank commented to me:

'It is unlikely that the banks will ever be nationalised, but it is certainly not impossible. We make very large profits and it is important that we should be seen to be prepared to put some of this income into worthwhile things like sport and the arts. The cricket sponsorship has been very successful from that point of view and also as a means of entertaining clients and saying thank you to our own employees.'

Below the level of first-class cricket, there is less likelihood, it seems, of sponsors sticking to the game over a long period of time. It remains to be seen how successful from the sponsors' viewpoint will be the two new sponsorships in Minor County cricket in 1983 – a knockout competition sponsored by English Industrial Estates for £15,000, and the Championship, sponsored for £5000 more than this by United Friendly Insurance. They may even switch from one competition to another. The whisky firm John Haig, for example, began by backing the village cricket championship, then switched to patronage of the national club knockout, originally started by *The Cricketer* magazine and the Midlands-based millionaire, Derrick Robins. Most club leagues now have a local sponsor, such as a group of local papers, a brewery or a sports goods firm.

On the whole there can be no question of the benefits of sponsorship in cricket, though it has inevitably created some problems that were not evident in the days when the local squire would write out a cheque to cover the financial losses which most counties made as often as not even before the slump of the 1950s. There are dangers which need to be watched. Let me conclude by pointing out the main ones.

The first is the increasing tendency for sponsorship of individual star players, which can lead to jealousies in a team game, as well as clashes with the sponsors of either the team itself or a particular competition. Inevitably, too, most of the riches available in the game are concentrated into the pockets of a few leading cricketers. The contrast between the annual struggles of the counties themselves and the average annual tax-free benefits of more than £50,000 underlines the fact that money is often more easily attracted by an individual than by a team or a club.

There is a temptation for cricketers to become mobile vehicles for advertisers, like tennis players with their rackets, shirts and shoes; motor-racing drivers and their cars; and now footballers, with the name of a company emblazoned across their shirts. Perhaps this is a necessary price to pay for the solvency of professional sport but to me it is an undesirable one. Cricket's guidelines on this 'visual advertising' are at present somewhat illogical. Any county ground in England has sponsored cars in the players' car park, with bold letters painted on the side advertising the donors. But strict limits have been laid down as to what is permissible in the way of insignia on shirts. Big money is now available to players for the use of certain equipment, especially bats, and several players have been guilty of being paid by more than one firm for the 'exclusive' use of their bats. Several of the Indian cricketers used bats in the 1983 World Cup which by contract they were not entitled to do.

Team sponsorships also have their problems. Most touring teams now have special agreements negotiated by agents on their behalf from which they all benefit, although some of the 'big name' individuals can resent these deals if they clash with their own commitments. Some players are also more responsible than others when it comes to returning the sponsors' generosity (albeit commercially motivated) by appearing at the right times in the right places. If all were as conscientious in this respect as England's wicket-keeper of recent times, Bob Taylor, cricket would never be short of commercial friends. But just a few of the younger players sometimes give the impression that the money will flow in without much co-operation on their part.

There is, finally, an unhealthily large dependence on tobacco companies in the area of first-class sponsorship. Benson and Hedges in Australia nearly withdrew from sponsorship of a Test in Perth in 1982 because of a proposal in the Western Australian parliament to tighten restrictions on cigarette advertising to the point where sports sponsorship would be forbidden. If such a move were to be made in Britain, which is possible – indeed probable in the not far distant future – county cricket would suddenly be bereft of a large slice of its income.

FIFTEEN

The Base
of the Pyramid

Cricket, in any developed country, has been aptly described as forming a pyramid. At the top there is Test cricket, and then there are several levels below, all based on the game as played by the young. Ultimately the quality of the game at the top will reflect the health of the game at the bottom.

As I mentioned in the last chapter, recent years have seen sponsors of school and club, as well as of first-class cricket, but it has always been the work of voluntary enthusiasts which has enabled cricket at these levels to flourish. Indeed, the last two decades have witnessed an intensification of the debate within the game about the need for correct coaching at an early age. Cricket is technically a difficult game and the instinct of most, if not all, boys who first pick up a bat is to hit across the line of the oncoming ball. We all learn that sooner or later the odds are against such a method succeeding. A ball travelling down a more or less straight line needs to be met with a more or less straight bat. But does it require coaching to teach this fundamental lesson, and the other basics of the game? Or will children born with a good eye, being natural mimics, not follow a good example almost without being told? If not, how did Don Bradman appear from the country town of Bowral, or Viv Richards and Andy Roberts from the one-time cricketing backwater of Antigua? In such places the game is handed down, as often as not, from father to son. But there is no doubt that if a boy does not get the opportunity to play the game in a reasonably organised way at school, his chances of developing into a successful cricketer are greatly reduced.

There have been several firm initiatives in the coaching field since the last war, emanating from Lord's and in particular from the efforts of H. S. Altham and G. O. Allen. In 1977 the Cricket Council of the United Kingdom set up an enquiry into youth cricket, against a background of concern about the decline of interest and participation by young people. As a result county cricket associations were urged to liaise more closely with schools and clubs to provide matches, coaching and facilities for young cricketers, especially in the sixteen to nineteen age-group. Keen players of this age were losing interest in the game, partly because there was no opportunity for them to play in organised matches outside school.

In many cases, of course, the problem lay, and still lies, in the schools themselves. Cricket requires at least some coaching, especially if there is no keen father to pass the game on, plus reasonable facilities. Once, this meant that a good grass pitch had to be maintained, something that could only be done by hard work from someone who knew what he was about. But the development of non-turf pitches in the last twenty years, and particularly in the 1980s when the production and sale of a wide choice of such artificial pitches has taken place, has enabled a youngster to play on a true surface without the fear of getting the ball smack in the eye every time he essays a text-book forward defensive.

The National Cricket Association is the organisation, based at Lord's, charged with the responsibility of encouraging better liaison between schools and clubs. Continuing the work of the MCC Young Cricketers Association, the NCA runs coaching courses for would-be teachers of the game both in schools and clubs. But there is not much they can do if teachers in schools are not able or willing to make the game part of the PE training of every child. In the village primary school which one of my sons attended for a time in the 1970s, cricket bats were banned by the headmistress on the grounds that they were dangerous.

The NCA coaches have developed various simpler games than cricket, played with a tennis ball, in which the skills of catching and hitting a ball can be learned and enjoyed, with

everyone getting a bat and a bowl. The chewing-gum manufac-
turers, Wrigleys, have in recent seasons sponsored a successful
and increasingly popular competition for primary schools
called Softball Cricket, with Trevor Bailey as the chief publi-
cist. Trevor firmly believes that one of the reasons for the West
Indian success in cricket is that youngsters in the island learn
the game first with a soft ball, often on the beaches. Imitating
his elders, the young West Indian runs in and hurls the ball
down as fast as he can to an uninhibited batsman able to hit the
ball fearlessly on the up.

Apart from non-turf pitches, the biggest development in
Britain in recent years has been the building of large indoor
sports halls in most large towns and cities, often with provision
for cricket nets. Many clubs now take part in indoor leagues,
playing a fast and enjoyable form of the game, which is almost
a mixture of cricket and squash.

It is a common belief that university cricket, which once was
an essential nursery of English Test cricketers, has declined,
both intrinsically and as a source of talent for county and Test
cricket. In fact one has to go back to the start of the period
under review, the early 1960s, when May, Cowdrey, Dexter,
M. J. K. Smith and Subba Row virtually carried the England
batting, to find as many players from Oxford and Cambridge
as those in contention for the national team twenty years on.
At the start of the 1983 season, for example, Tavaré, Marks,
Edmonds, Pringle and Ian Greig were all among the top twenty
names in the notebooks of the England selectors. In addition,
men like Fowler and Allott, both products of Durham University, emphasise that, though the provincial universities do
not play first-class cricket, several of them help to supply the
counties with new talent.

Nevertheless, there is a noticeable contrast between the five
names from the Oxbridge teams of recent times mentioned
above and the comparable group from the 1960s. Four of
those five captained England and three of them, May, Cowdrey and Dexter, were indisputably world-class batsmen. Of
the later group, all but Tavaré are more or less all-rounders,

reflecting the emphasis in limited-overs cricket on being able to do a bit of everything. Only Tavaré and Edmonds could come under serious consideration for a 'world' classification, though Pringle still has time. Whether this suggests a paucity of outstanding talent in English cricket generally in the early 1980s, or a decline in university cricket itself, is a moot point. But any decline would appear to have been neither so great, nor so comprehensive, as the difficulties besetting Fenner's and the Parks in the last twenty years might have indicated. For even in these days of studious attention to academic work, when to seek employment without an exam qualification is usually the height of optimistic folly, the university game is in remarkably robust health. The grounds are almost as beautiful as ever they were, batsmen still take the occasional hundreds off county attacks – though not quite as often as they did at Fenner's just after the war – and Cambridge even beat Lancashire fair and square in 1982. If the universities are no longer producing Mays and Cowdreys, no one else is either.

On the other traditional fields of play, league cricket in the northern half of England has gone on much as before, though nowadays most of the games are conducted on a limited-overs basis. Consequently those clubs employing professionals now go first not for bowlers but for batsmen. This is just another proof of the change which has been wrought by limiting the overs. Once, the emphasis was on bowling the other team out. Now it is on containing them, then 'knocking off the runs'.

Duncan Worsley, the Oxford captain who opposed Mike Brearley in the latter's days as Cambridge skipper, has played most of his cricket in the Bolton League where he now plays as professional for Heaton. 'The greatest change', he says, 'is in the standard of the bowling. You get very few good bowlers now and certainly you never come across a proper spinner.' This may account for the fact that Sonny Ramadhin, still a professional in the same league, picks up a bagful of wickets each season with unpredictable wrist spin at an age when most cricketers are boring their grandsons with tales of their exploits years ago.

Ray Illingworth has also bemoaned the steady decline in bowling standards in Yorkshire league cricket. The application of limited-overs cricket to the leagues is, he is convinced, the main reason for the slowdown in the production of raw fast bowlers and subtle spin bowlers who once queued up at Headingley each April, hoping for a trial.

The institution of league cricket itself is not in question in the north: in the south, it is. In the last twenty years a movement begun in south London, largely through the foresight of the former England left-hander, Raman Subba Row, has spread to almost all clubs, be they town or village. Leagues have sprung up like toadstools all over the south and those who at first resisted the idea, in the belief that the traditional 'friendly' cricket of old had done them well enough for a century or more, soon found that their traditional fixtures were in danger of being lost unless they themselves joined their local leagues.

Having played club cricket in the south for ten years before the league began in my particular area, West Surrey, I am not convinced that the game has changed much as a result of the fact that most games on Saturdays are now played for points rather than simply for pleasure – and honour. It was always true that the captain of the side held the key to the way that the game was conducted. There were some dull, unenterprising games before league cricket just as there are now many exciting and enterprising ones. The majority of the leagues in the south do not, in any case, have a limit to the number of overs, so it is still up to captains to time their declarations, if necessary, realistically. On the whole, unenterprising teams do not win leagues, but it is unfortunately true that the number of positive captains has grown fewer. The majority settle in the field for the dreaded policy of keeping the other side quiet by using medium-paced bowlers. Yet any batsman knows that when he first gets to the wicket what he least wants to face is either someone genuinely quick, or a spinner who really turns the ball.

As in first-class cricket, the standard of fielding has improved considerably in the club game over the last two decades. Other less desirable features of the first-class game have also, inevitably, filtered down to lower levels. Even before Trevor Chappell bowled his infamous last-ball 'sneak' against New Zealand, a club in Surrey had been expelled from a knockout competition because a bowler used exactly the same expedient in a similarly tense situation. Dissent at umpires' decisions has also become more common. In 1981, Graham Turner, chairman of the Club Cricket Conference, found it necessary to issue a warning and a plea to the 10,000 league cricketers then playing in the CCC area alone, to stop what he saw as a growing trend towards unsportsmanlike behaviour. Later, in 1983, E. W. Swanton, in his capacity as chairman of the committee running *The Cricketer* Cup, the successful knockout competition for old school clubs, was obliged to issue a strong warning to these traditional upholders of the spirit of cricket, that needling of players in the field, swearing, and open dissent at umpiring decisions, was spreading. His warning followed two years after a letter by the President of MCC, Hubert Doggart, to all match managers of MCC out-games against schools and clubs, to buck up the over-rate to twenty overs an hour at least. As captain for many years of two such games I was disagreeably surprised to find that one needed to make a special effort to keep up to such a rate. The tempo of the game has undoubtedly slowed as captains have become fussier and bowlers, unconsciously no doubt, have copied their counterparts in first-class cricket, taking their time as they walk back and after following-through.

In addition to the proliferation of leagues in the south of England, knockout cups, often sponsored locally, have also become more common. These range from evening matches played over a few overs each side to national competitions such as the National Club Knockout and the National Village Championship. As mentioned in the last chapter, it has been little problem for *The Cricketer* magazine, which originally organised both competitions, to find new sponsors for them. The finals are now held on the same weekend at Lord's each year. For village cricketers, albeit relatively sophisticated ones these days, to have the chance to play at the most famous cricket ground of all, is incentive enough for any participant, additional sponsorship or not. Findlay Rea, an erudite and enterprising septuagenarian who has organised the Whitbread Village Championship for ten years, stated categorically last year:

'In 1983, village cricket is flourishing, with a higher standard of cricket, better grounds and facilities, greater enthusiasm and a wider appeal than ever before.'

Of the Whitbread competition he said:

'Many clubs are stimulated by it (650 in 1983) and it provides new fixtures and lasting contacts.'

Undoubtedly this competition in particular has been a spur to many village clubs to take their cricket more seriously and improve their own facilities. The great majority of even the smaller clubs now have their own bar, for example: bad news for the village pubs, perhaps, but an essential way of making profits for the club, which in turn keeps membership fees for most village clubs down to a modest £5 or £10 a year.

The majority of clubs have now become aware that because of inadequate facilities at many schools, increasing pressure from exams and the earlier end to the summer term now customary (not to mention a growing emphasis on other summertime athletic pursuits), their responsibility to provide cricket for keen youngsters has grown. Colts sections of many large clubs have expanded and flourished, mainly through the efforts of a few dedicated individuals. To give but one example, Dr John Dew, who played briefly as an amateur for Sussex, started coaching sessions in midweek for a few local primary and secondary schoolboys in 1958. Now some 150 boys can be seen spread over Horsham's ground every Thursday evening throughout the summer, and almost all have the chance to play in matches, at six different age levels, against other Sussex clubs.

In Sussex there is also a remarkable voluntary effort known as the Sussex Junior Cricket Festival, an annual event which has spread to include a multitude of holiday matches and even tours. Such efforts supplement the increasingly well-organised supply of holiday cricket provided by the English Schools Cricket Association and the National Association of Young Cricketers. ESCA and *The Cricketer* jointly organise a Colts Trophy for schools, sponsored originally by Esso and now by the Lord's Taverners charity. More than 1500 schools now take part in the competition, which first involves boys of under fourteen in county competitions, then the qualifiers play the following year in the national competition for boys under fifteen. Winners have come from both the leading public schools and from grammar and comprehensive schools.

The NCA, again with sponsorship from the Lord's Taverners, Commercial Union and others, runs competitions at under thirteen, under fifteen, under sixteen and under nineteen age-levels. Finance from the Lord's Taverners and Wrigleys also enables them to give grants towards coaching courses, the provision of visual aids such as films and videos (with help from the Nat West Bank, a superb new coaching video was produced in 1983), and representative tours. The majority of England's recent Test caps have previously been on official England schools tours to countries such as India, Sri Lanka, Australia and West Indies – valuable experience which their predecessors would never have had.

It is perhaps a little sad for the premier club itself, MCC, that, having set in motion these developments after the last war and organised the conference of youth cricket organisations at Lilleshall in 1951 – out of which developed the advanced coaching courses, first run by the MCC Youth Coaching Adviser, Harry Crabtree – they should now have ceded responsibility for club and youth cricket in England. It was MCC, of course, who decided to start the NCA and who, until recently, supplied much of the financial backing for its activities. Alas, there has been much political in-fighting at Lord's involving MCC, the NCA and the TCCB.

Changes in the role of MCC were studied by a special working party set up in 1982, after criticism of the facilities provided for the club's 18,000 members, and of its financial administration by committees which tended to be self-perpetuating. The working party firmly concluded that it was right for MCC, the private club with a public function, to continue to act as guardian of the Laws of the Game, and to provide the secretary and chairman of the ICC as well as the venue for important matches. But like many county clubs (and much of British government generally?) the committee was considered too large and the sub-committees too numerous for efficient management of the club's affairs. Several far-reaching proposals were made to reduce committee work, make decision-making easier and introduce fresh blood. The idea that the president should be elected for one year only (and elected solely by his predecessor) was also considered to be in need of review. It was a classic demonstration of the continuing British ability to evolve gently rather than to resist all change until a revolution occurs.

In many ways this has been true of all the changes in non-first-class cricket between 1963 and 1983. Interest and participation in the game in all four countries of the British Isles has seldom been higher or more healthy. So long as young cricketers continue to receive help from their elders, and the spirit of friendly cricket is maintained even in a more competitive age, amateur cricketers, in the United Kingdom at least, can look beyond 1984 with few qualms.

SIXTEEN

The Future

'Striving to better, oft we mar what's well.'
These words from King Lear might have been pondered a little more often before changes were made to some aspects of cricket in the restless years between 1963 and 1983. But though it is true that one timeless quality of cricket lies in its relative gentleness and subtlety, in an age of increasing violence, rapid change and emphasis on instant action, it is also true that cricket is bound to continue to reflect society's changes. The game must continue to adapt, or die.

Some new ideas – for example a two-divisional County Championship or a Championship played over four days – can only be tested fairly over a long period. What I should most like to see, however, is a greater willingness on the part of cricket administrators to test new ideas, or old ones resuscitated, before they are let loose on the game. The ideal vehicle for giving a fair trial to sensible experiments would be the Scarborough Festival in September. The matches at this famous finale to the first-class season have always been played more or less seriously, but they are never life-and-death affairs. With the presence of top-class cricketers but no points at stake, there would be a chance to gauge how practical certain ideas for improving the game really are.

Amongst the experiments worth trying are a smaller seam on the ball to encourage spinners, or, a law permitting only one new ball per innings in order to counter the polishing effect of fertilised outfields which preserve the shine on the ball longer than before.

To give the batsmen more chance against ever more athletic

and intimidatory fast bowling there should also be trials with a longer pitch. In November 1983 two Tests began on the same day, one in Perth, one in Ahmedabad, in which both Australia and West Indies chose four specialist fast bowlers and not a single specialist spinner. In order to make the longer pitch simpler – and more acceptable to players brought up on measurements which have remained unchanged since the earliest days of the game, when the old agricultural chain, twenty-two yards, was adopted – the experiment should begin with bowlers having to deliver from level with the stumps; if the front foot lands completely over the bowling crease, a no-ball should be called.

Jon Henderson of Reuters calculated in 1981 that if the present twenty-two yards, introduced when men were much smaller on average than they are now and before overarm bowling was legal, were to be increased to twenty-two metres, the batsman would have 9.27 per cent more time in which to react to a ball travelling at ninety mph. In fact, to push the bowler back to the bowling, as opposed to the popping, crease, would be asking him to bowl from only four feet (1.22 metres) further back. That would hardly be a drastic change and bowlers would very quickly get used to it. Incidentally, but equally important, it would give umpires as well as batsmen fractionally longer to react.

It is quite illogical that the height and width of the wicket have been changed since the early days of the game, but not the length of the pitch. It is equally illogical that the 1980 Code of Laws should have laid down shorter measurements for junior cricket, thus recognising the crucial relationship between human physique and the length of the pitch, yet failed to take account of the scientific fact that men are much taller than they were throughout the world a hundred years ago. In addition, modern nutrition and physical training methods have made all athletes, including fast bowlers, capable of greater speeds sustained over longer periods. We are talking only of split seconds: the difference between a ball travelling twenty metres as opposed to twenty yards, at ninety mph, is 0.44 of a second!

But one often talks of a bowler suddenly 'finding an extra yard of pace'. More time must inevitably give a batsman more chance against extreme speed. It would also make the fast bowlers work a little harder and, if there is still a spinner left in the team, it would give him more air space to work in and therefore, presumably, more chance to beat the batsman by flight.

Another possible experiment to reduce not only the domination of fast bowlers, but also their frequent use of bouncers, would be to have a line across the pitch a little to the batsman's end of the middle. The length of the line would be determined by the umpires at the start of the match, depending on the pace of the pitch. The square-leg umpire would call no-ball for any delivery pitching on the bowler's side of the line. Moreover, as with other no-balls and wides, the extra would in future count against the bowler's analysis. This latter idea was tried successfully in the 1983–84 season in Australia and India. The problem with the line across the pitch is that it would make little difference to bowlers like Joel Garner, who can 'bounce' the ball almost off a good length.

Even more revolutionary would be a Law allowing only three nominated bowlers in any team to run up more than ten yards. This would impose a maximum of three fast bowlers and more or less guarantee the use of at least one spin bowler. It is a simple and apparently foolproof solution, although admittedly an artificial one.

Intimidation by fielders has also increased since the introduction of helmets, which have given Dutch courage to men fielding close in on the leg side. It is not feasible, now that helmets have started to be worn, for a ban to be made on their use by fielders; otherwise guilt would be felt by the legislators if a helmetless fielder were to die from a fractured skull. (This has happened in non-first-class cricket, while at the highest level there have been several near misses in the last twenty years. Glamorgan's Roger Davis was clinically dead for a few seconds after being hit on the head when fielding close in on the leg side, and in 1982, the Indian captain, Sunil Gavaskar, had his leg broken when it was hit at close range by a full-blooded square-cut from Ian Botham.) As for batsmen, there have been many more hit on the head since the introduction of helmets which fractionally slow reactions and encourage hook shots which would not otherwise have been attempted. But it is commonsense to protect the head.

If, therefore, it is wrong to deny protection to either fielders or batsmen, there is no alternative to artificial legislation. I would experiment with another white line, this time to keep close fielders from encroaching beyond a reasonable distance: say six feet from the edge of the cut portion of the pitch. Otherwise the logical progression of present trends is for close fielders dressed like American footballers, standing literally inches from the batsman. Fielders are there to stop and catch the ball, not to intimidate. When the spirit of the law is constantly broken, legislation, alas, is the only solution.

The proliferation of matches at first-class level has made life even harder than it always was for the groundsman, and there is much to be said for Tom Graveney's contention that all county one-day games should be played on an artificial cricket pitch. The best of these surfaces, which have been exhaustively researched and tested, especially by the Nottinghamshire County Council's playing fields officer, Peter Dury, have all the properties of a good turf wicket, without the same need for maintenance or the susceptibility to wet weather. Graveney believes that the lack of good pitches is the main reason for the relatively lower scoring by all teams in Test cricket in the last ten years.

Rain has always been the bane of cricketers and covering of pitches has recently been much improved. In England pitches used not to be covered in first-class games and as a result matches could change course as suddenly as a shower could blow up. Covered pitches have taken away the possibility of a 'sticky' wicket, a wet pitch under the influence of hot sun, which used once to provide such fun for bowlers, such a challenge to batsmen and such a spectacle for onlookers.

On the other hand, covered pitches and, in Test matches in

England at least, bigger tarpaulin covers which protect most of the square, have given spectators more chance of seeing cricket once the rain has stopped. At Edgbaston there is now a huge tarpaulin on a motorised roller which covers most of the ground, an expense which Warwickshire believe has already been recouped in terms of time saved for cricket, but which no one else has yet copied. The attitude of players and umpires is also crucial when weather intervenes. Their general attitude is more often than not that they will play only when they are able to do so without fear of slipping. Yet every week in Britain tens of thousands of club cricketers cheerfully play on through showers or drizzle. If run-ups have to be restricted and everyone has to take care, it matters little. The great thing is to be getting on with the game.

Professional cricketers must force themselves to take the same attitude, if they are to keep their public. One notorious example was the Test at Lord's in 1980 held to celebrate the centenary of the first Test in England at The Oval. A deplorable insensitivity on the part of players and umpires to the spirit of the occasion prevented play on the Saturday when, with a few concessions made, it was perfectly possible. The day was sunny and the ground full but tempers understandably rose as, even on this special occasion when the result did not matter, umpires and captains refused to take any risks with their own safety – risks taken regularly by amateur cricketers. In a series for the Ashes such caution and stubborn disregard for the public *might* have been more understandable.

One recognises the difficulties facing the umpires but, even if they consider conditions unfit for play, they should always allow it to start if the fielding captain is prepared to play in wet conditions, or the batting captain when the light is deemed unfit. I should like to see this written into the next Code of Laws and, meanwhile, into every set of tour regulations. One day, perhaps, we shall have a national stadium where, as at the Houston Astrodome in Texas, it is possible to push a button when the rain starts and thus shut out the weather with a sliding roof.

Another experiment worthy of further trial is the West Indian proposal that an lbw should be allowed to a leg-break bowler bowling right-arm over, or left-arm round, if the ball has pitched outside the leg stump but has turned to strike the pad in line with the wicket and, in the opinion of the umpire, would have hit the wicket. There is neither logic nor justice in allowing lbws to bowlers who can seam or spin the ball in from outside the off-stump, but not from the leg. When the Law was changed in 1937, after a two-year trial, to allow lbws for balls pitching outside the off stump, the fear was that bowlers would negatively 'attack' the batsman's legs. But there would be no point in doing this if lbws remained impossible for balls pitching outside the leg stump if delivered by a left-arm over-the-wicket bowler, or a right-armer going round. From the 'opposite' angle it is not so easy to bowl negatively. Somehow the leg-spinner must be saved, and this would undoubtedly help.

On wider matters than legalities, the players and administrators of tomorrow are going to have to heed the lessons of the last twenty years. Too many overseas players in England have on balance deprived young, home-grown players of valuable experience. Therefore there must be no going back on the plans to limit the counties to one overseas star from the mid-1980s on.

Continuing efforts must be made to resolve the problem of South Africa's isolation from Test cricket. At the very least, leading cricket administrators who have not done so should go to South Africa to judge the country and its cricket themselves.

The vigilance against slow over-rates must continue, by the insistence on a minimum number of overs in a day's play: in Test cricket in England 96 overs has proved about right, but that number should not be reduced any further, and, as already mentioned, I should like to see four-day Tests with a minimum of 110 overs each day.

The proliferation of Tests and one-day internationals must cease. Saturation point has already been reached and further acceleration, to the detriment of the players' sharpness and enthusiasm and the increased apathy of crowds, can only be avoided by an agreement between all the Test-playing countries to limit themselves to a reasonable maximum of matches each year.

The evil of crowd hooliganism, which has so bedevilled association football, must be nipped in the bud by cricket administrators. Selective opening of bars or, if necessary, no alcohol on sale at all, the provision of three or four mounted police along the boundary's edge, and, if necessary, high wire fencing, are all nettles which may well have to be grasped soon.

Players who transgress, through foul temper publicly displayed or undue pressurising of umpires, must be heavily punished. Myth though it may be in some ways, cricket's reputation for fair play must be jealously guarded by the twentieth-century Elizabethan as it was by the nineteenth-century Victorian. It is as true in 1984 as it was in 1962 that it is the attitude of the players and the captains that will determine the health of cricket, at whatever level it is played. Good pitches to play on, enterprising captaincy, and an affection for cricket by those who play it will protect the greatest game from the 'sordid and dishonourable'.

Even Lord Harris would not, I believe, completely despair of his cherished game as it looks towards the twenty-first century. But we would all do well to contemplate again this poetical reiteration, published in *Punch*, of cricket's essential character, all the more valuable in the age of rush and violence:

Cricket's too slow
And beret-crowned, bright-shirted in his car
The film-like youth spoke thus and sped afar,
And left me to September sunset glow,
To summer ghosts that tarried at the game
A gentle-dying yet eternal flame.
Cricket is slow,
Thank God for that, when fever drives the mind
Through burning miles we leave more miles behind,

To build new hells and let the beauty go.
Let's hold this picture, though the seasons pass –
The sunlit field, the shadows on the grass,
And keep it slow,
With brief swift moods – the catch, the stolen run –
A gracious game, with fickle ebb and flow,
That breeds good fellows, kind and quiet-faced,
Not bound upon the chariot wheels of haste.

INDEX